From
Life
to
Death

From
Life
to
Death

❖

Richard Allen Brooks

Library of Congress Control Number: 2011900724
ISBN: Hardcover   978-1-4568-5336-5
                 Softcover   978-1-4568-5335-8
                 Ebook   978-1-4568-5337-2

This book was printed in the United States of America.

To order additional copies of this book, contact:
Xlibris Corporation
1-888-795-4274
www.Xlibris.com
Orders@Xlibris.com
89915

CONTENTS

This book is dedicated to the memories of my mother, ETHEL MARIE BROOKS FLEET, and my longtime friend JOSEPH BERNARD DAVIS. His death inspired my first poem, LIFE.

FOREWORD

If you are seeking perfect rhyme and meter, go no further because you are about to read the wrong book of poetry. If, however, you are seeking thoughtful introspection, reasoned thought and query, interrogatory and response, then proceed to read this book, for that is just what is in store for you in this first compilation of the poetic expressions of Richard Allen Brooks.

No one can fully understand or appreciate the works of another person. We each bring to our interpretation our own set of experiences through which we must view the work. We have not lived the author's life, tribulations, exalts, despair, disappointments, or jubilations.

Our interpretation of the author's work is thus a skewed vision of what the author intended in the original meaning of the work, even if only slightly, and it must be so in order to fit within the confines of our own personal experience, which must always be different from that of the author, if not in kind then in degree.

Starting with "A Friend Indeed" that offers encouragement, "Your Name" tells of living your life but never obtaining the goals you've set for yourself, while "The Falling Snow" was a quiet time—after the loss of mother dear, "sitting on the steps of my younger sister's home, just looking out the window at the flakes landing here and there." Another one, "How Sad This Day," expresses a loss after losing another loved one and then there is "Between Atlantic and Pacific," an awareness of those who died during World War II and a memorial dedicated to them.

Additionally, the reader must be advised that Mr. Brooks, throughout his life, has been a tireless giver of his time and energy to the advancement of mankind in every manner at his disposal. As much joy as his work has brought him, it has also contained bitter returns through many people who mistook his willingness to be of assistance as a weakness and, thus, resulted in significant pain and disappointment being experienced by Richard.

There are many other themes running through this work. However, there are three predominant and recurring themes, which the reader will be confronted with—Richard's profound sense of loss on the death of his mother, a search for direction, and the passing of time.

This work should be read with deliberation. Much of what it has to offer cannot be appreciated through casual, mindless reading. However, if you take the time to think about not just what is being said, but why it is being said and the message that is being conveyed in each poem, you will come away from this book greatly enriched in your understanding of the significance of love, loyalty, commitment, compassion, and understanding not just for your fellow man but for yourself.

—Marilyn V. Joyner

LIFE

LIFE, I BREATHE INTO IT.
LIFE, I GREW WITH IT,
VISUALIZING MY DREAMS IN IT.
LIFE HASN'T ALWAYS GIVEN ME THE
OPPORTUNITIES TO FULFILL THEM IN IT.
LIFE, I TRY AND I TRY AND TRY TO PREPARE FOR IT.
LIFE GIVES ME MANY JOYS AND HAPPINESS IN IT.
LIFE, MY DREAMS BECOME REALITIES IN IT.

LIFE, YET IS NOT ALWAYS GENTLE AND KIND IN IT.
LIFE CAN BE PERPLEX AND DEALS ME
MANY DISAPPOINTMENTS IN IT.
LIFE CAUSES ME TO FACE THE HATRED,
THE STRESS, THE PAIN, AND THE ANGUISH
OF MY TORMENTED SOUL IN IT.

LIFE, ALONG ITS EXHAUSTING PATH,
I BEGIN TO LOSE HOPE IN IT.
LIFE, WITH COURAGE, WITH FAITH,
WITH ENDURANCE, AND WITH TRUST,
I REGAIN MY DESIRE IN IT.

LIFE PROVIDES ME MANY SIGNALS IN IT.
LIFE, SUDDENLY, I AM GONE FROM IT,
AND NOT TO BE NO MORE
FOR ME IN IT.

ca. 1998

A FRIEND INDEED

WHEN YOU TRY TO DISCUSS,
WHEN YOU ARE WILLING TO CONFER
AND SHARE YOUR KNOWLEDGE,
THAT'S A FRIEND INDEED.

WHEN YOU PROVIDE INFORMATION,
WHEN YOU OFFER ADVICE
IN AN EFFORT TO ASSIST OTHERS,
THAT'S A FRIEND INDEED.

WHEN YOU PRESENT SOLUTIONS,
WHEN YOU GIVE INTERPRETATIONS
FOR THOSE THAT LACK UNDERSTANDING,
THAT'S A FRIEND INDEED.

WHEN A FRIEND IS DOWN,
WHEN YOU GIVE ENCOURAGEMENT
SO THEY CAN MOVE FORWARD,
THAT'S A FRIEND INDEED.

WHEN ONE IS IN DESPAIR,
WHEN YOU PROVIDE THEM HOPE
TO BRIGHTEN THEIR DAY,
THAT'S A FRIEND INDEED.

WHEN ONE IS IN DISARRAY,
WHEN YOU GIVE THEM COMFORT
TO HELP THEIR CONTENTMENT,
THAT'S A FRIEND INDEED.

WHEN A FRIEND ASKS FOR HELP,
WHEN YOU MAKE SACRIFICES
TO GIVE THEM ASSISTANCE,
THAT'S A FRIEND INDEED.

WHEN A FRIEND IS LEFT HOMELESS,
WHEN YOU TAKE THEM IN
TO PROVIDE SHELTER FROM THE COLD,
THAT'S A FRIEND INDEED!

PERHAPS, JUST MAYBE,
YOU WILL RECEIVE
JUST ONE, MAYBE, JUST ONE,
"THANK YOU"

ca. 2002

ADVENTUROUS LIVING

REMINISCING WHILE GAZING AT THE SEA
ALL THE ADVENTUROUS LIVING KNOWN
FROM HERE AND FROM THERE,
DINNERS AT WORLD'S BEST,
ALL PART OF ADVENTUROUS LIVING.

CLASSICAL, POP, JAZZ, AND FOLKLORE,
BALLETS, CONCERTS, SYMPHONIES,
OPERA, PLAYS, AND THEATRICAL EVENTS,
ALL PART OF ADVENTUROUS LIVING.

TRAVELED THROUGHOUT THE SOUTH,
FROM MAINE TO FLORIDA IN THE EAST
TOURED UP AND DOWN THE WEST
ALL ACROSS THE NORTH AS WELL,
VENTURED INTO CANADA AND MEXICO TOO,
ALL PART OF ADVENTUROUS LIVING.

IN AND OUT OF THE COUNTRY,
EXPERIENCING VARIED CULTURES,
EVEN ON OTHER CONTINENTS,
SO FAR, ASIA, AUSTRALIA, AND EUROPE
AND THEIR LIFESTYLE WAYS,
ALL PART OF ADVENTUROUS LIVING.

THIS WAS NEVER EXPECTED
ALL JUST A PART OF ADVENTUROUS LIVING.

ca. 2010

ALASKA—DREARY AND GLOOMY

ALL HUMAN PREPARATION FULLY FULFILLED.
UNAWARE, DREARY AND GLOOMINESS AWAITED
THE LONG ANTICIPATED CRUISE HAD ARRIVED.
QUIETLY THE REALIZATION LOOMED GREATLY.

HOWEVER, NATURE WAS TOTALLY IN CONTROL.
DAY IN, DAY OUT, AS THE CRUISE CONTINUED,
DAILY THE CLOUDS AND RAIN PREVAILED,
CAUSING DREARINESS AND GLOOM TO PERSIST.

DISEMBARKING INTO THE BLEAK, DISMAL CITIES
LEFT A FEELING OF FAINT AND WEAK SPIRITS,
LESS DESIRED TO BEAR THIS LONG-AWAITED CRUISE
RETURNING HOME COULD NOT COME FAST ENOUGH,
FROM ALASKA—DREARINESS AND GLOOMINESS.

ca. 2009

AUSTRALIA—THE BRIDGE BEYOND

THE VIEW FROM THE OPERA HOUSE STEPS
OFFERS A TREMENDOUS, PICTURESQUE VIEW.
IN THE DISTANCE IS AUSTRALIA'S AMAZING BRIDGE,
AN AWESOME, BREATHTAKING VIEW OF THE HARBOR.
TO THE RIGHT, THE CIRCULAR QUAY FERRY TERMINAL
WITH SHIPS AND SAILBOATS MAKING THEIR PASSAGES,
SOME SHIPS TO THE LEFT, SOME BOATS TO THE RIGHT.

THE BLUE-GREEN WATER QUIETLY SIMMERING,
THE SUN INTENSELY PIERCING FROM HIGH ABOVE,
WHILE MANY SIGHTSEERS STROLL AROUND,
ALL TYPES OF CAMERAS CLICKING EVERYWHERE.

YET THE SERENE TRANQUILLITY LEAVES PEACEFULNESS.
BEYOND, BUILDINGS APPEAR TO BE STANDING ERECT.
DIRECTLY ACROSS FROM THE OPERA HOUSE IS THE
RENOWNED, FAMOUS ROYAL BOTANIC GARDENS
THAT INCLUDES THE GOVERNMENT HOUSE.
ALL THIS GIVES THE IMPRESSION OF PAYING
HOMAGE TO SYDNEY, AUSTRALIA.

ca. 2010

BARBARA'S JOURNEY

MANY START PURSUING THEIR LIFE'S JOURNEY,
CROSSING THE WIDE AND DESOLATE PLAINS,
HAVING TO CLIMB THE TREACHEROUS MOUNTAINS,
FINDING THEMSELVES IN THE VALLEY OF SHEAR DESPAIR.
BARBARA TOOK LIFE'S JOURNEY WITH DETERMINATION,
INCLINED TO TRAVEL HER AWESOME PATHWAY.

BARBARA ENCOUNTERED EXHILARATING EXPERIENCES:
GAINING FRIENDSHIPS, AFFILIATIONS, PARTICIPATION,
PLEASURES, JOYS, AND HAPPINESS ALONG THE WAY;
ALSO, ENDURED THE ANGUISH, SORROW, AND PAIN
EXPERIENCED WHILE TRAVELING HER LIFE'S JOURNEY.

WHEN BARBARA'S JOURNEY WAS NEARING ITS END,
LITTLE DID HER FAMILY AND FRIENDS REALIZE
SHE WAS REACHING THE CONCLUSION OF
HER LIFE'S JOURNEY WITH US HERE ON EARTH,
EXTRAORDINARILY COURAGEOUS UNTIL THE END!

BARBARA'S JOURNEY HAS TAKEN HER HOME ON HIGH.
NOW, SHE HAS GONE TO HER FINAL RESTING PLACE.
SOONER OR LATER, WE WILL ALL JOIN HER THERE.
UNTIL THEN, WE WILL REMEMBER HER COMPASSION,
HER GENTLENESS, UNDERSTANDING, HER WARMTH,
AND SUPPORT ON HER EARTHLY LIFE'S JOURNEY.

SO, GOOD-BYE, DEAR BARBARA, WE WILL MISS YOU,
ENJOY YOUR HEAVENLY JOURNEY OF JOYFUL BLISS.

December 2004

BARON O'BRIEN

BARON O'BRIEN, A QUIET RULER OF HIS PRINCIPALITY,
A LEADER WHO IS NOT EASILY PERCEIVED,
TO APPROACH IS WITH PRECARIOUSNESS.
WHEN NECESSARY, HE IS PERSPICUOUS.
HE WILL OFFER NO ABSOLUTE PALLIATE,
SELDOM WILL YOU FIND HIM PERTURBED.

BARON O'BRIEN IS NOT ONE FOR PROTRACTION.
THERE HAVE BEEN CONCERNS ABOUT HIS PACE,
EVEN THOUGH HE MAY APPEAR PALTRY,
HE IS NOT KNOWN TO REGARD PROMPTITUDE.
HOWEVER, HE IS AWARE OF HIS PRECIPITANCY
FEW INSTANCES, THERE IS A STRONG PASSION.

BARON O'BRIEN WILL NOT BE NO ONE'S PLOY.
NEVERTHELESS, THERE IS A DEGREE OF PENSIVENESS.
ON OCCASIONS, HE WILL REVEAL HIS POTENCY.
HE OFFERS SUGGESTIONS THAT ARE PLENTEOUSLY.
HIS PRESENTATIONS CAN APPEAR PONDEROUSLY.
BARON O'BRIEN ARISES FOR EVENTS PORTENTOUS.
THUS, YOU ARE TO BE RECOGNIZED, BARON O'BRIEN.

ca. 2004

BETWEEN ATLANTIC AND PACIFIC

HERE IN THE MIDST OF THE WWII MEMORIAL
CONTRIBUTING TO THIS POWERFUL NATION
BETWEEN ATLANTIC AND PACIFIC OCEANS
A NATION OF MANY STATES
A NATION OF NUMEROUS TERRITORIES
A COUNTRY CLAIMED TO HAVE BEEN FOUNDED
A COUNTRY TAKEN FROM NATIVE AMERICANS
A COUNTRY BUILT OF BLOOD, SWEAT, AND TEARS.

NOW, WATCHING THE WATER FOUNTAINS FLOWING
OBSERVING PILLARS REPRESENTING THE STATES
THOSE PILLARS REPRESENTING THE TERRITORIES
NOTICING ENGRAVED NAMES UPON GRANITE PILLARS
NOTICING COUNTLESS TOURIST ENTHRALLED
GAVE AN INDESCRIBABLE TONE OF SADNESS.

AWARENESS OF THOSE THAT DIED DURING THE WAR
A MEMORIAL DEDICATED TO THEIR REMEMBRANCE
FOR OUR NATION TO REMAIN
THE LAND OF THE FREE,
HOME OF THE BRAVE,
BETWEEN ATLANTIC AND PACIFIC OCEANS.

OCTOBER 2004

BLACK BROTHER

BLACK BROTHER, "DO YOU KNOW
WHERE YOU ARE GOING?"
"HELL, IF I KNOW."
"NO ONE EVER GAVE ME DIRECTIONS.
I HAVE KEPT MOVING IN CIRCLES,
WHERE, I DON'T KNOW."

"I ASKED FOR GUIDANCE:
SOME OUTRIGHT REFUSED
SOME ANSWERS WEREN'T CLEAR
SOME JUST DAMNED CONFUSIN'
SOME GAVE WRONG DIRECTIONS.
THEY WANTED ME TO REMAIN LOST."

"YOU THINK THEY WOULD BE TRUTHFUL
SOME ARE NOT TO THEMSELVES,
SOME DON'T KNOW HOW,
SOME AREN'T TO ANYONE ELSE,
SOME HAVE ATTEMPTED TO DECEIVE.
SOME OUTRIGHT WILL LIE."

"YOU MUST WATCH WHAT SOME SAY,
YOU MUST WATCH WHAT THEY DON'T SAY,
YOU MUST READ BETWEEN THE LINES."
SO, TELL ME, BLACK BROTHER,
"WHERE ARE YOU GOING?"

"SOME CAN'T FOLLOW DIRECTIONS,
SOME DON'T KNOW WHERE THEY'RE GOING,
SOME WON'T SAY, THEY DON'T UNDERSTAND,
SOME PRETEND THEY'RE ON THE RIGHT PATH."
PERHAPS, MY BLACK BROTHER,
"IT'S INDICATIVE YOU FOLLOW THE RAFT."

ca. 2002

BRIGHT LIFE, DIMMED LIFE, DARK LIFE

WHAT HAS HAPPENED TO THE BRIGHT LIFE?
WHERE HAS IT GONE?
WHAT WENT WRONG?
WAS I TOO BUSY ENJOYING THE BRIGHT LIFE?
PURSUING THE GOOD TIMES, FUN, AND GAMES.
ENJOYING THE BRIGHT LIFE!

DIM LIFE SLOWLY CREPT UPON ME.
IGNORED ALL THE WARNINGS SIGNS,
CRISIS BEGAN TO OCCUR.
THERE WERE ISSUES LEAVING A BLUR,
UNTIL THE DIM LIFE BESIEGED ME.
EAGERLY, RAN TOWARD THE BRIGHT LIFE.
ALL TO NO AVAIL!

WHAT HAS HAPPENED TO THE DIMMED LIFE?
WHERE DID IT GO?
WHAT WENT WRONG?
SHOULD HAVE PREPARED FOR THE DARK LIFE!
HINDSIGHT REVEALS A WASTE OF TIME.

DARK LIFE HAS QUIETLY ARRIVED.
WHAT A TROUBLED LIFE PREVAILS,
ONE DILEMMA, AND THEN ANOTHER,
JUST HOW BLEAK CAN IT BECOME?

IN THE MIST OF THIS DARK LIFE,
BODY SHELL ATTEMPTS STEADFASTNESS.
ALL THE JUICES HAVE EVAPORATED,
NO ROOM FOR INSPIRATION,
ALL HOPE HAS DISSIPATED.

FACE THE NUMBNESS OF THIS DARK LIFE.
REALITY CONCLUDES THE AWARENESS,
NOT ANOTHER DAY MAY COME FORTH.
THE BRIGHT LIFE AND DIMMED LIFE GONE,
TROUBLING REALIZATION LEAVES DESPAIR
THAT ONLY PRESENT IS DARK LIFE.
DARK LIFE WILL SOON CEASE TO EXIST.

ca. 2002

CECELIA AKA TRINKET

CECELIA, AKA TRINKET, MIRACULOUSLY
APPEARED ONCE UPON A LIFETIME;
FROM HER LUSTROUS BEGINNING,
YOU MET A PERSON THAT FILLED
MANY A WORDS IN THAT LIFETIME,
PROVIDED MANY A TASK ON TIME.

CECELIA, AKA TRINKET, HAS BEEN THERE,
VISIBLE FOR ALL KEENLY TO OBSERVE,
NEVER AN OBSTRUCTIONIST,
SUBTLE IN HER DELICATE PERCEPTION,
ALWAYS EXTREMELY GENEROUS,
REGARDLESS WHAT STAGE OF LIFETIME.

CECELIA, AKA TRINKET, IN HER
YOUNG AND PROMISING LIFETIME,
AVAILABLE FOR SOCIAL CREATIONS,
ENCOURAGED, REQUIRED STIMULATION,
THERE OFFERING HER ABILITIES TO ALL,
NO MATTER THEIR STATION IN LIFETIME.

CECELIA, AKA TRINKET, WAS THERE,
INTO A YOUNG ADULT OF LIFETIME,
FOR INTELLECTUAL INTERACTIONS,
PROVIDED EXHILARATING ADVENTURES,
PRESENT FOR CONDOLATORY OCCASIONS,
VOLUNTEERING SUPPORT AND ASSISTANCE.

CECELIA, AKA TRINKET, NOW HAS
ENTERED A MATURITY OF HER LIFETIME,
OFFERING HER EXTENSIVE EXPERIENCES
FIRST FOR ONE, THEN FOR ANOTHER,
NEVER ASKING FOR ANY COMPENSATION,
NEVER SEEKING ANY FORM OF SENSATION,
SHE IS TRULY, ONE IN A LIFETIME.

ca. 2003

CHANGING OF THE GUARDS

IT IS INEVITABLE, THERE IS NO ESCAPING.
IT IS INEVITABLE, TIME BRINGS CHANGES.
IT IS INEVITABLE, CHANGING OF THE GUARDS.
IT IS INEVITABLE, AGING REQUIRES REPLACEMENT.
IT IS INEVITABLE, DISCOVERIES PROVIDE OPPORTUNITIES.

EDUCATION PROVIDES NEW KNOWLEDGE.
ABILITIES OFFERS ADDITIONAL CHALLENGES.
EXPERTISE EXTENDS EFFICIENT EVALUATIONS.
ADDITIONAL SKILLS PRESENTS NEW AWARENESS.
EXPERIENCES OFFER CHANCES FOR STRENUOUS REVIEWS.

IT IS INEVITABLE, NOTHING REMAINS FOREVER.
IT IS INEVITABLE, THIS DAY WILL ULTIMATELY END.
IT IS INEVITABLE, THAT CHANGES WILL CONTINUE.
IT IS INEVITABLE, MANY WILL NOT ULTIMATELY BE READY.
IT IS INEVITABLE, THE CHANGING OF THE GUARDS WILL COME.

ca. 2007

DAME JOHNSON

THIS GRANDE LADY IS

DIS-TIN-GUISH-A-BLE IN HER
      DEMURE DELIVERIES.
      DELIGHTFUL AND DAZZLING,
      THE LADY IS DEFINITELY
      A DIVA.

A-STON-ISH-ING-LY ADMIRABLE
      AND ADD HER AC-CLA-MA-TIONS.
      SHE IS AMAZINGLY AFFECTIONATE.
      THE LADY'S ADDITIONALLY
      AFFABLE.

MAG-NAN-I-MOUS, MAGNIFICENT,
      AND MERITORIOUS,
      HER METHODOLOGY IS
      METICULOUS.
      THE LADY IS MERELY MARVELOUS.

EX-TRAOR-DI-NAR-I-LY EX-EM-PLA-RY,
      EXCITING, AND EXPLICIT,
      SHE IS EXCEEDINGLY EXCELLENT.
      THE LADY IS EVEN EXQUISITE!

JU-DI-CIOUS-LY JUST AND JOLLY,
      SHE JOGS IN HER JOURNEYING.
      THE LADY IS JOYOUSLY JUBILANT.

OS-TEN-SI-BLY OP-U-LENT AND ORDERLY,
  SHE IS OBSERVED AS OBJECTIVE.
  THE LADY IS OVERWHELMING.

HON-ES-TY AND HEARTENING, A HIP HEROINE,
  SHE HAS HUMILITY.
  THE LADY SHOWS HER HEREDITY.

NOT-ED-LY NATURAL AND NIMBLE,
  SHE IS NATIVE-BORN.
  THE LADY IS A NEOCOSMIC.

SO-PHIS-TI-CAT-ED-LY SUAVE AND SINCERE,
  SHE IS SURELY SENSITIVE.
  THE LADY IS A SAVVY STYLIST.

OUT-STAND-ING-LY OVERT AND OB-VI-OUS,
  SHE IS OVERWROUGHT.
  THE LADY IS OBLIGING.

NO-TA-BLE NOBLY IN *NOUVELLE VAGU,*.
  SHE POSSESS *NOUVEAUX* RICHES.
  THE LADY'S A TRUE NOBLEWOMAN.

              THIS IS WHY THE LADY IS CALLED,
              THE GRANDE DAME OF ALL,
              "DAME JOHNSON"

ca. 2000

DO I TRUST?

I TRUST THE GENTLE FRAGRANCE THAT FILLS THE AIR.
I TRUST THE SWEET SMELL OF A WARM SUMMER NIGHT.
I TRUST THE BEAUTY OF ROSES THAT GROW.
I TRUST THE SILENCE OF THE CALM SEA.
I TRUST THE GOLDFISH THAT SWIM IN MY TANK.
I TRUST THE DEPTH OF MY INNER SOUL.

BUT, DO I TRUST ANYTHING ELSE?
I DON'T KNOW.
DO I TRUST THE PLACES I GO?
I DON'T KNOW.
DO I TRUST ANYONE?
I DON'T KNOW.
IF I DO, I WILL LET YOU KNOW.

ca. 1999

EMPEROR KING

EMPEROR KING NOBLY STANDS BEFORE ME.
THIS NOBLEMAN HAD QUIETLY APPROACHED
TALL, HANDSOME, AND APPEALING GENTLEMAN,
EXTRAORDINARILY FINE AS WELL AS GRACIOUS,
HIS DISTINGUISHED PRESENCE IS ELECTRIFYING,
EYE CONTACT IS EXCEEDINGLY WARM,
THE EPITOME OF ARISTOCRATIC EXCELLENCE.

EMPEROR KING CONTINUES TO PRESENT HIMSELF
WITH AN ALARMING MAJESTIC MANNER,
HE IS ALWAYS REGAL IN HIS PRESENCE.
SPEAKS WITH SINCERITY IN HIS TONE,
INSTANTLY CAUSING YOUR AWARENESS,
ALERTING YOU, YOU ARE SAFE WITH HIM.
A TRUE ELITE, AN ARISTOCRAT NOBLEMAN.

EMPEROR KING OFFERS POWERFUL SOVEREIGNTY;
HIS FORTITUDE IS OF MAGNETIC POWER,
CAUSING UNQUESTIONABLE IMMOBILITY,
LEAVING YOU AN IMPETUS DESIRE,
BEFORE HIM TO KNEEL REVEALINGLY,
WHEN HE TOUCHES YOU IN SUPPORT,
YOU FEEL YOUR DREAMS CAN BE REALIZED.

EMPEROR KING OF MASTERFUL QUALITIES,
YOU KNOW HE IS GENUINELY SUPREME.
YET HIS AUTO CHARISMA IS MESMERIZING.
VIRTUES NOT OFTEN SEEN FROM ANYONE,
EXHIBITING THE STATESMANSHIP OF A KING,
TRULY PRAISEWORTHY OF THIS ACCLAIM,
HAIL, EMPEROR KING.

ca. 2005

FAREWELL, THOSE WE KNEW

WHEN WE ARRIVE HERE,
NO ONE COMES FOREVER.
YET WHEN ONE EXPIRES,
WE SUCCUMB TO SADNESS AND PAIN.
A TREMENDOUS MELANCHOLY OVERWHELMS
FAMILY, RELATIVES, LOVED ONES, AND FRIENDS.
PUBLIC FIGURES CAUSE MORE SORROW IN THE END.

LATELY, THERE HAVE BEEN KNOWN PERSONS,
ENTERTAINERS, MAKING THEIR TRANSITIONS
NOW, BEGRUDGINGLY REFLECTING BACK,
MANY HAVE LEFT US WITH THEIR VOID.
PAUL, CARL, GREGORY, AND VIRGINIA,
CAUSING MANY PAINFULLY AFFECTED,
EVEN AS WE REMINISCE ABOUT OTHERS.
ALSO BARRY, ISABEL, LINCOLN, AND RAY
HAVE CAUSED MANY OF US GREAT AGONY.

NO MATTER HOW MANY MEET THEIR DEMISE,
EXPERIENCES OF ACUTE PAIN NEVER CEASE
ALTHOUGH THEY ARE IN ANOTHER PLACE,
WE SAY, FAREWELL, THOSE WE KNEW.

ca. 2004

GIVE YOUR LIFE A CHANCE

YOU DIDN'T ASK TO BE BROUGHT HERE
YOU DIDN'T HAVE CONTROL
YOU ALLOWED OTHERS THEIR CHANCE
NOW, YOU DO HAVE AUTHORITY
FOLLOW YOUR MIND
LISTEN TO YOUR HEART
GIVE YOUR LIFE A CHANCE.

BLOCK OUT ALL CONDEMNATION
IGNORE SOCIETIES' ACCUSERS
CAREFULLY ANALYZE OTHERS WISHES
AVOID FRIENDS' DEMANDS
FOCUS ON YOUR DESIRES
THEN, REALIZE YOUR DREAMS
LISTEN TO YOUR HEART
GIVE YOUR LIFE A CHANCE.

ca. 2004

GO

AT THIS TIME
    I RISE TO LEAVE
        WHERE IN THE HELL TO,
        I DON'T KNOW.
            YET REALIZE I MUST GO.

ALL THIS TIME
    MADE NO PLANS TO ROLL,
        WHICHEVER WAY THE WIND BLOWS
        SEARCHED HIGH AND LOW
            YET REALIZE I MUST GO.

ALTHOUGH THIS TIME
    THE JOURNEY WILL BE SLOW,
        CREATING MY PATH AS I GO
        GIVING TIME TO FIND MY GOAL,
            YET REALIZE I MUST GO.

ALL THIS TIME
    SHOULD HAVE PREPARED,
        IF I PLAN TO GROW
        WHERE TO, I DON'T KNOW.
            YET REALIZE I MUST GO!

ca. 2003

GOOD-BYE FOREVER

"GOOD-BYE"
HOW MANY TIMES HAVE I SAID IT?
HOW MANY TIMES HAVE YOU HEARD IT?
EACH TIME I HAVE DEPARTED,
I HAVE SAID, "GOOD-BYE"
EVERY TIME YOU LEFT ME,
WE HAVE SAID, "GOOD-BYE"
AT THE CLOSING OF THE DAY, "GOOD-BYE"
TEMPORARY UNTIL WE MET AGAIN.
WHEN WE LEFT ONE ANOTHER,
PARTING WAYS UNTIL THE NEXT TIME,
IT WAS ALWAYS A "GOOD-BYE."
NOW, THE "GOOD-BYE" WILL BE FOREVER.
THE SMELL OF MANY FRAGRANT FLOWERS,
I LOOKED UPON YOUR SERENE, GENTLE FACE
I REALIZED YOU ARE FINALLY AT PEACE
LOOKING UPON YOUR REPOSED BODY,
IT IS "GOOD-BYE" FOREVER.

ca. 2004

HE LISTENED

HE STOOD, HE LISTENED,
LEANING AGAINST THE COUNTER.
HE SPOKE, I LISTENED.
I SPOKE, HE LISTENED.
FIRST TO ONE, THEN TO THE OTHER
AMIDST THE CROWDED ROOM.

WE THEN SAT.
HE SPOKE OF INCIDENTS ENCOUNTERED
I LISTENED.
I SPOKE OF SITUATIONS EXPERIENCED
HE LISTENED.
HE SPOKE OF OCCASIONS AFTER ANOTHER
AS HE RECOUNTED,
I LISTENED.
I RECALLED ONE PREDICAMENT, THEN ANOTHER
HE QUIETLY SAT THROUGH IT ALL.
HE LISTENED,
AS ONLY HE COULD DO.

ca. 2004

HOW COMFORTING

IN MOMENTS OF PAIN, YOU'RE HERE,
YOU HAVE ALWAYS BEEN HERE,
HOW COMFORTING.

WHEN YOU GENTLY TOUCH ME,
AND YOU HOLD ME CLOSELY,
HOW COMFORTING.

YOU SPEAK SOFTLY IN MY EAR,
SAYING, YOU WILL ALWAYS BE HERE,
HOW COMFORTING.

IN BAD DAYS, YOU WERE HERE,
WHEN YOU SHOW YOU CARE,
HOW COMFORTING.

YOU HAVE MADE SURE I WASN'T ALONE
WHEN MAKING MY DECISIONS,
HOW COMFORTING.

WHEN RECEIVING ACCOLADES, YOU'RE HERE,
TIMES OF CELEBRATIONS YOU HAVE BEEN HERE,
HOW COMFORTING.

AT TIMES, MY DAYS TURNED INTO NIGHTS,
WHEN NIGHTS WOULD NOT END, YOU WERE HERE.
HOW COMFORTING.

WHEN LOST, YOU HAVE FOUND ME,
WHEN NOT AT MY BEST, YOU WERE THERE,
HOW COMFORTING.

WHEN SHIVERING FROM THE COLD,
YOU'RE HERE TO WARM ME,
HOW COMFORTING.

UNABLE TO SPEAK, YOU FELT MY DESIRES,
AND YOU SPOKE FOR ME,
HOW COMFORTING.

WHEN YOU'VE GIVEN ME STRENGTH,
IN LOSING A LOVED ONE, YOU'RE HERE.
HOW COMFORTING.

WHEN MY WEEKS TURNED INTO MONTHS,
MONTHS TURNED INTO YEARS, YOU WERE HERE.
HOW COMFORTING.

WHEN ALL ARE GONE, YOU ARE HERE,
HOW COMFORTING,

HOW COMFORTING.

ca. 2003

HOW SAD THIS DAY

WHAT'S A MOTHER TO SAY?
WHAT'S A MOTHER TO DO?

HOW'S A MOTHER TO HANDLE HER PAIN?
HOW'S A MOTHER TO DEAL WITH HER ADVERSITY?

WITH WHOM CAN A MOTHER SHARE HER GRIEF?
WITH WHOM CAN A MOTHER SHARE HER SORROW?

WHY HASN'T ANYONE OFFERED A SHOULDER?
WHY HASN'T ANYONE PROVIDED THEIR SUPPORT?

WHEN WILL THIS STRAIN DASH?
WHEN WILL THIS SHADOW PASS?

WHERE CAN THIS MOTHER TURN?
WHERE CAN THIS MOTHER RUN?

HOW SAD THIS DAY!
SO, PLEASE, LORD,
LET HER ENDURE ANOTHER DAY.

ca. 2002

HOW WONDROUS!

THIS PICTURESQUE VIEW FROM MY BEACH SEAT
AT THIS MAGNIFICENT BREATHTAKING RESORT,
BENEATH PALM TREES ON THE SANDY BEACH,
THE SHIMMERING CLEAR BLUE WATER,
SHIPS MEANDERING TO AND FRO,
THE DISTANT CLOUDS TOUCHING THE SEA
WHILE COVERING THE LIGHT BLUE SKY.
HOW AMAZING, HOW WONDROUS!

THE SUN RAY PENETRATES TO BELOW,
GRAINY SAND REACHES TO THE SEA,
ROCKS AND PILLOWS DEEPLY DRILLED,
HOLDING BACK THE ERODING EARTH,
BEHIND THE ROCKS, PILLOWS, AND SAND,
VARIOUS COMPLEXES OF ALL SHAPES,
SIZES, AND IMAGINABLE COLORS STAND
HOW AMAZING, HOW WONDROUS!

YET FARTHER BACK IN THE DISTANCE,
AMONG ALL THIS MAJESTIC BEAUTY,
MOUNTAINS EMERGE TOWARD THE SKY.
BIRDS FLYING WITHOUT STRETCHED WINGS,
WHILE THEY ACTIVELY SEEK THEIR PREY,
ALL THIS, AS A GENTLE BREEZE BLOWS,
HOW AMAZING, HOW WONDROUS!

JUST BEHIND ME STANDS A RESTAURANT.
THERE, THE BAND JUBILANTLY PLAYS ON,
MANY ARE SWIMMING, OTHERS SUNBATHING,
SOME INDULGING IN THEIR FAVORITE DRINKS,
ON THE BEACH BEFORE ME, MANY MERCHANTS,
CUSTOMERS BARGAINING FOR THEIR PRODUCTS,
HOW AMAZING, HOW WONDROUS!

AT CORAL BAJA, SAN JOSE DEL CABO, MEXICO.

ca. 2003

I HEAR THE ALARM

THERE IS A TIME FOR EVERYTHING.
WE DON'T TAKE NOTICE,
I HEAR THE ALARM,
I KNOW ITS SOUND.

WE'RE BUSY DOING OUR THING.
BUSY WITH ANYTHING,
I HEAR THE ALARM,
I KNOW ITS SOUND.

WE'RE BUSY PLAYING AROUND.
BUSY MAKING OUR ROUNDS,
I HEAR THE ALARM,
I KNOW ITS SOUND.

WE WILL NEVER BE ON TIME!
BUSY WITH OUR TIME.
I HEAR THE ALARM,
I KNOW ITS SOUND.

IT'S LETTING US ALL KNOW,
DON'T WORRY ABOUT ANY HARM,
IF WE JUST STAY CALM.
I HEAR THE ALARM,
I KNOW ITS SOUND.

ca. 2000

I WONDER

I WONDER,
WHY THERE IS SO LITTLE LOVE?
YET WE TALK AND SING OF LOVABILITY.

I WONDER,
WHY THERE IS SO MUCH ANTIPATHY?
YET WE PREACH AFFECTIONATE.

I WONDER,
WHY THERE IS SO MUCH DISHONESTY?
YET ALL CLAIM THEIR TRUTHFULNESS.

I WONDER,
WHY THERE IS SO MUCH DISHARMONY?
YET SOME SWEAR THEY ARE HARMONIOUS.

I WONDER,
WHY THERE IS SO MUCH PREJUDICE?
YET MOST ASSERT THEY'RE NOT BIAS.

I WONDER,
WHY THERE IS SO LITTLE TRUST?
YET THEY'LL CHARGE TRUSTWORTHINESS.

I WONDER,
WHY THERE IS MUCH CONCERN FOR ANIMALS?
YET LITTLE ATTENTION IS GIVEN OUR CHILDREN.

I WONDER,
WHY THERE IS MUCH HUNGER TODAY?
YET WE ARE GREAT HUMANITARIANS.

I WONDER,
WILL I EVER KNOW?

ca. 2003

I WONDER WHY?

I WONDER WHY
MANY PEOPLE ASK QUESTIONS,
YET THEY KNOW THE ANSWERS?

I WONDER WHY
PARENTS ASK WHAT'S GOING ON
WITH THEIR CHILDREN?

I WONDER WHY
TEACHERS ASK WHAT IS THE PROBLEM
WITH SOME OF THEIR STUDENTS?

I WONDER WHY
SOCIETY ASKS WHAT IS WRONG
WITH THE YOUNG GENERATION?

I WONDER WHY
BUSINESSES ASK WHAT IS THE PROBLEM
WITH THEIR EMPLOYEES?

I WONDER WHY
COMMUNITY LEADERS ASK WHAT IS WRONG
WITHIN THEIR COMMUNITIES?

I WONDER WHY
POLITICIANS ASK WHY THEY'RE HAVING PROBLEMS
GETTING ACROSS TO THEIR CONSTITUENCIES?

I WONDER WHY
PEOPLE ASK WHAT IS THIS WORLD COMING TO?
WITH ALL THE PROBLEMS OF TODAY

THE TRUTH OF "I WONDER WHYS" IS
NO ONE WANTS THE ANSWERS
SINCE THEY ALREADY KNOW.
I WONDER WHY?

ca. 2003

IF I WAS THERE

ALL THE EXCITEMENT SURROUNDING ME
THE SOLEMNNESS OF THE MAGNIFICENT OCCASION
WE TREMBLED WITH NERVOUSNESS
THEN, THERE WAS THE SOUND OF MUSIC
THROUGH ALL THE MANY PEOPLE
CAME THE MELODIC, GENTLE SOUND.
YOUR VOICE, AS YOU BEGAN TO SING
MY KNEES BECAME EXTREMELY WEAK.
IT SEEMED, AS I MOVED SLOWLY TOWARD YOU,
OUR EYES MET WITH AN EXPRESSION,
THIS SONG WAS FOR ONLY ME.

ALL I COULD DO WAS HOLD MY COMPOSURE
AS MY HEART DID ITS OWN GYMNASTICS,
CAUSING ME TO SUDDENLY RECOGNIZE
THIS WAS MY FIRST TRUE LOVE.
NOW TIME HAS RAPIDLY PASSED
IF I WAS THERE
TO REALIZE THAT FEELING ONCE AGAIN.
ONLY, IF I WAS THERE
WHAT EXCITEMENT FOR LOVE AGAIN.
WHAT JOY, IF I WAS THERE.

ca. 2004

IN THE CHARM OF SPRINGTIME

IN THE CHARM OF SPRINGTIME,
       SITTING IN TOTAL AMAZEMENT
              OF GOD'S CREATIONS FOR MANKIND,
                     WATCHING THE RAYS OF THE BRILLIANT SUN
                            BEAMING ALL OVER THIS AWESOME LAND.

IN THE CHARM OF SPRINGTIME,
       LISTENING TO THE CHIRPING OF BIRDS
              WHILE GLEEFULLY GLIDING AROUND,
                     FOCUSING ON THE ARRAY OF COLORFUL FLOWERS,
                            SMELLING THE SWEET FRAGRANCE OF
                            BLOSSOMS.

IN THE CHARM OF SPRINGTIME,
       NOTICING THE BEAUTY OF MANICURED LAWNS
              GIVING OFF A REDOLENCE OF AN EARTHY SCENT
                     COMPATIBLE IN FILLING THE DELICATE NOSTRILS
                            AWARE OF NUMEROUS TREES' PLEASANT
                            AROMA.

IN THE CHARM OF SPRINGTIME,
       FEELING THE SOFT, GENTLE, AND CAREFREE BREEZE
              AS IT CARESSES TENDERLY AGAINST THE BODY,
                     GIVING A RESOUNDING, VIBRANT EXHILARATION
                            SILENTLY PRAISING THIS CHARMING
                            SPRINGTIME.

                                                    ca. 2007

IN THE MORNING

IN THE QUIET OF THE MORNING,
I SIT AND WONDER,
DO I NEED SOMEONE'S CAFÉ
OR JUST A CUP OF COFFEE?

EVERYTHING IS STILL.
IT GIVES MY MIND TIME TO CHILL.
WHAT WILL ANOTHER DAY GAIN?
PERHAPS, A LOT OF THE SAME!

WHATEVER I DO TODAY,
I DON'T WANT TO BRING NO SHAME,
BUT RATHER GAIN SOME FAME.

THEN, I CAN SAY,
IN THE QUIET OF THE MORNING,
ANOTHER DAY WAS NOT IN VAIN.

ca. 2000

INDULGENCE OF MY ILLUSION

TREMENDOUSLY CONFIDENT,
EVEN SELF-ASSURED,
DECEIVES NO ONE BUT SADLY MYSELF,
THOUGHT I HAD MY LIFE UNDER CONTROL
ALTHOUGH,
NOT SURE OF MANY ISSUES IN LIFE,
NEVER REALIZED I WAS NOT IN AUTHORITY,
CIRCUMSTANCES' SUBTLETY REVEALED DIFFERENTLY.

REVELATIONS BROUGHT FORTH MY FLAWS,
HOWEVER, I PAINFULLY HAD TO ACCEPT,
ALLOWING MY SUBLIMINAL STATE TO OPERATE
BLINDED BY INFLUENCES OF MY ILLUSIONS.
NOW, IN THIS ABYSS, WHAT APPEARS NEXT?
A DILEMMA THAT HAS BECOME INSOLVABLE
ALL DUE TO INDULGENCE OF MY ILLUSION.

ca. 2005

JOHN JOHN

JOHN JOHN, A CHARISMATIC, DEBONAIR YOUNG MAN,
A MAN OF UNFINISHED ILLUSTRIOUS CHALLENGES,
I DID NOT KNOW THIS EXTRAORDINARY LAD,
NEVER HAD THE OPPORTUNITY TO CONVERSE,
NEVER MET THIS EXEMPLARY GENTLEMAN,
NOT EVEN IN HIS ASTONISHING PRESENCE.
YET FELT JOHN JOHN, AS HE WAS CALLED,
SEEMED CLOSER THAN SOME I HAVE KNOWN,
CLOSER THAN SOME I HAVE TALKED WITH,
EVEN CLOSER THAN SOME I HAVE MET.

RESULT OF HIS SUAVENESS ON TELEVISION,
RESULT OF NUMEROUS NEWSPAPER ARTICLES,
RESULT OF THE MANY MAGAZINES' COVERAGE,
THE EXTENSIVENESS PIERCED ME TREMENDOUSLY.
LEAVING ME ULTIMATELY TOUCHED BY HIS DEMISE,
MY PRECISE INSIGHTFULNESS CAUSED ME TO REALIZE,
JOHN JOHN'S UNDERTAKINGS WERE NOT COMPLETED,
WHEN HIS EARLY TRAGEDY OF EXPIRY TIME OCCURRED
ALONG WITH HIS LOVELY WIFE AND SISTER-IN-LAW,
A TRUE AMERICAN TRAGEDY REALIZED BY ALL.

ca. 1999

LADY ANNIE

SINCE LADY ANNIE'S TRANSITION,
MY EMOTIONS HAVE REMAINED SUBMERGED,
AN INABILITY OF EXPRESSING MY FEELINGS
HAS LEFT ME UTTERLY SPEECHLESS,
DISAVOWING THE TREMENDOUS HURT,
DENYING THE VAST EMPTINESS FELT,
CONCEALING MY AGONIZING PAIN,
SUPPRESSING MY DISMAL SORROW,
TIME HAS QUIETLY TRANSCENDED.
THESE ADVERSITIES FERVENTLY REMAIN
WHILE THE PRESENCE OF PAIN CONTINUES.

SINCE LADY ANNIE'S EXPIRY,
I HAVE EXPLORED THE INNER SELF,
EXPERIENCING UNPARALLELED INSIGHT,
CONVEYING MY PRIVATE THOUGHTS,
MY EVOCATION REMINDS ME,
EVEN AS TIME HAS BEEN PROTRACTED,
OF THIS MIRACULOUS ENLIGHTENMENT.
YET THERE'S NOT AN EXCLAMATION
TO DEAL WITH THESE ANGUISHED FEELINGS.

SINCE LADY ANNIE'S DEMISE,
ACKNOWLEDGING, BECOMING WHO I AM
GREATLY AS A RESULT OF HER PRESENCE,
THE RESULTS OF HER SAGACIOUSNESS,
HER UNDERSTANDING TOUCHED ME DEEPLY.
THE SURMOUNTABLE DIRECTION SUGGESTED,
THE IMMEASURABLE ADVICE PROVIDED,
THE EXTRAORDINARY SUPPORT OFFERED,
REMAIN FOREVER VIVIDLY IN MY MIND.

LADY ANNIE, THROUGH MY SUBJECTIVE EYES,
PROVIDED HOPE TO ALL SHE ENCOUNTERED.
HER KINDNESS TRULY IMMEASURABLE,
SHE POSSESSED A GRACEFUL DEMURE.
HER EXQUISITE CHARM RADIATED ELEGANCE,
HER LOVE WAS UNQUESTIONINGLY GENUINE,
HER WIT ASTONISHINGLY REFRESHING,
INSIGHTFULNESS REVEALED HER CONVICTIONS.
SHE STRONGLY WOULD FIGHT FOR HER BELIEFS,
YET SHE COULD BE AMAZINGLY GENTLE.

NOW LADY ANNIE'S GONE, LEAVING A VOID.
SHE IS STILL SORROWFULLY MISSED.
SHE WILL ALWAYS FOREVER BE REMEMBERED.

ca. 2003

LADY MARILYN'S GOWN

DURING OUR MORNING COFFEE,
TELL ME ABOUT YOUR EXQUISITE GOWN.

"THIS GOWN OF MINE
IT IS THE RESULT OF A WEDDING
IT IS SIMPLY ADORABLE
IT IS BEAUTIFUL AND DAZZLING
IT IS ELEGANT AND MAGNIFICENT
IT IS GORGEOUS AND CLASSY
WHEN I WEAR IT,
IT MAKES ME FEEL FANTASTICALLY SASSY."

"THIS GOWN OF MINE
HAS STRAIGHT LINES WITH LITTLE FUSS,
ADORNED WITH A BOW THAT GATHERS DUST
AND SLEEVES THAT ARE PERFECTLY PUFFED."

"THIS GOWN OF MINE
WORN AS A COCKTAIL HOST
LEFT ME THE PARTIES' TOAST
I GOT THEIR ATTENTION,
THAT WAS MY INTENTION."

"THIS GOWN OF MINE
IS CAUSE TO WEAR AGAIN AT ITS PRICE,
ONLY AFTER MY HIPS LOSE A SLICE."

"THIS GOWN OF MINE
OH, WHAT THE HELL,
I WILL DO WELL TO GET INTO
THIS GOWN OF MINE
SO AGAIN I CAN SHINE."

LADY MARILYN WITH A FLAIR
RAISED HER HEAD IN THE AIR,
AS WE CONTINUED SIPPING OUR COFFEE.

ca. 1999

LET ME REST

FOR ALL THE CONTINUOUS HOURS,
DURING THE TREMENDOUS DAYS,
THROUGH THE NUMEROUS WEEKS,
IN ALL THE MULTITUDE OF MONTHS,
THROUGHOUT THE HORRENDOUS YEARS,
I STEADILY WORKED AT MY DESK.
NOW, LET ME REST.

IN THIS INDETERMINATE TIME SPAN,
TRAVELING ALL AROUND THE WEST,
I HANDLED MY ACTIVITIES WITH ZEST,
I HAVE PARTAKEN IN MANY A FEST,
I HAVE DISAVOWED THE MESS,
ALWAYS ATTEMPTED TO DO MY BEST.
NOW, LET ME REST.

AT TIMES, LEAVING MY COMFORT NEST,
SOME USED ME FOR THEIR CHESS,
OTHERS HAVE BEEN GREAT PESTS,
CAUSED ME HOLD CLOSE TO MY VEST
MANY PUT ME THROUGH THEIR TEST,
ATTEMPTING TO KEEP ME FROM MY QUEST.
NOW, LET ME REST.

AS I LOOK BACK AT THE PAST,
OFTEN INVITED TO BE THE GUEST
HAVE BEEN PLACED IN VARIOUS CASTS,
AS MY NATURE CAUSES ME TO TRUST,
FAMILY MEMBERS HAVE CAUSED DISGUST,
FRIENDS ATTEMPTED TO USE ME FOR LUST,
ALWAYS RECEIVING THEIR DUST.

YET I REMAINED JUST
NOW, LET ME REST.

ca. 2002

LORD JENKINS

AWE, THERE STANDS LORD JENKINS.
WELL, SHOULD I APPROACH
OR PERHAPS, RETREAT?
OOH, I HAVE A CHANCE TO CONVERSE,
OR MAYBE, REMAIN SECRETIVE.
HAW, IF HE INQUIRES OF ME,
NOW, SHALL I DISCLOSE
TO PLEASE HIS SPECULATIVENESS?
WOW, WHAT IS IT ABOUT HIM
THAT LEAVES ME IN A DITHER?

IT'S NOT HIS MERE PRESENCE,
OR CAN THAT BE?
IT'S NOT HIS PHYSICAL STATURE,
OR PERHAPS IT IS?
HMM, THERE IS RESERVATION.
IT'S NOT HIS SUPPOSITIONS OF OTHERS,
OR LIKELY IT IS.
IT'S NOT HIS SOCIAL MANNERISM,
OR POSSIBLY IT IS.
IT'S NOT HIS ALLUSIVE DISPOSITION,
OR COULD IT BE?
IT'S NOT HIS DISTINCTIVE STYLE,
OR MAYBE SO.
NAY! PROBABLY, HIS EFFECTUAL NOBLENESS.

I HAVE SEARCHED FOR ANSWERS,
YET HIS MYSTIQUE PREVAILS.
GEE, PERCHANCE, IT COULD BE ME,
MY OVERACTIVE INTUITIVENESS.
STILL, THE AMBIGUITY REMAINS.
POSSIBLY, I KNOW!
HE IS AS COMPLEX AS ME.
THEN, TRULY I WILL NEVER KNOW
HOW TO APPROACH
LORD JENKINS.

ca. 2000

MASS CONFUSION

THIS TROUBLED MIND IS WORKING OVERTIME.
THE WAY IT IS RUNNING MUST BE A CRIME.
LIGHTS GOING ON EVERY WHICH WAY,
CAUSING EACH AND EVERY CELL TO SHINE
MOLECULES RUNNING TO AND FRO,
THOUGH SOME WILL EVEN STOP ON A DIME
NONE OF THESE MOLECULES OFFER
CHEMICAL CORRECTNESS FOR SANITY
ATOMS FREE TO ROAM WITHOUT A NUCLEUS,
PREVENTING THAT WHICH WILL SAVE MY KIND
HENCE, NOTHING ON THIS ROTARY
IS RHYTHMICAL AT ANYTIME
THUS, CAUSING ALL THIS MASS CONFUSION
IN MY DEMENTED MIND.

ca. 2004

MERCY, MERCY ME

MERCY, MERCY ME
WHAT SHALL I DO TODAY?
HOW CAN I PREVENT FURTHER DECAY?

MERCY, MERCY ME
LOOK AT THIS ENVIRONMENT
OUR ATMOSPHERE NEEDS IMPROVEMENT

MERCY, MERCY ME
THE RIVERS ARE SEVERELY POLLUTED
MANY OF THE ROADS NEED REPAIRING

MERCY, MERCY ME
OUR TRANSPORTATION IS APPALLING
TOO MANY CARS FOR INADEQUATE ROADWAYS

MERCY, MERCY ME
OUR COMMUNITIES ARE DEPLORABLE
EVEN OUR SCHOOLS ARE NOT COMPATIBLE

MERCY, MERCY ME
THE RICH DON'T GIVE A DAMN ABOUT THE POOR
CHILDREN PLACED IN GROUPS AS HERDS

MERCY, MERCY ME
WHAT SHALL I DO TODAY?
HOW CAN I PREVENT FURTHER DECAY?

ca. 2003

MY CELLOPHANE PRINCE

MY CELLOPHANE PRINCE,
ARE YOU SATISFIED AS AN ANONYMITY?
IT IS NOT CLEAR.
DEMAND YOUR RIGHTFUL DIGNITY.
PURSUE YOUR RIGHTS AND LIBERTY.

MY CELLOPHANE PRINCE,
ARE YOU SATISFIED IN YOUR WELL?
IT IS NOT CLEAR.
IT'S NOT EASY FINDING TIME TO DWELL.
APATHY SHOULD NOT SWELL.

MY CELLOPHANE PRINCE,
ARE YOU SATISFIED IN YOUR SHELL?
IT IS NOT CLEAR.
REALIZE YOU ARE NOT COMPELLED
TO BE OBSCURE THIS SIDE OF HELL.

MY CELLOPHANE PRINCE,
IT IS CLEAR.
NO MORE TRANSPARENCY, PRETENSE.
LEAVE YOUR FROG-LIKE BEHAVIOR.
RELEASE THOSE HIDDEN CRAVENS.
STRETCH OUT, FIND YOUR HAVEN.

MY CELLOPHANE PRINCE,
IT IS CLEAR.
DON'T BECOME SOMEONE'S PILL.
ALLOW YOUR DREAMS TO FULFILL.
INDECISIVENESS LEAVES DREAMS UNFULFILLED.
BECOME THE PRINCE, YOU WILL.

MY CELLOPHANE PRINCE,
IT IS CLEAR.
ASSERT YOURSELF, TAKE CONTROL.
FOLLOW YOUR VISION, GO ON PATROL.
LET THE WORLD REALIZE YOUR ROLE,
MY CELLOPHANE PRINCE.

ca. 2000

MY DAD

HERE, AMIDST MY REFLECTIONS
THROUGH THE MANY TEARS,
I HAVE MOMENTS OF HAPPINESS
I HAVE MOMENTS OF GREAT SADNESS
WHILE MUDDLING THROUGH PREPARATIONS
OF ARRANGEMENTS FOR MY DAD'S FINALITY.

YOU ASK ME, HOW DO I FEEL?
LUCKY, I WILL TELL EVERYONE.
HAVING MY DAD EIGHTY-EIGHT YEARS
ALWAYS THERE WHEN I NEEDED HIM.
BEEN HERE WHEN MY DAD NEEDED ME.

NOW, THAT HIS TRANSITION HAS COME,
HIS LEAVING ME HAS CAUSED SORROW.
HIS DEMISE HAS CAUSED ME EMPTINESS
YET THIS FINALITY GIVES ME RELIEF
KNOWING THAT MY DAD IS NOW AT PEACE.

TRINKET

ca. 2004

MY FEAR

I RAISE MY VOICE IN FEAR.
CAN'T EXPRESS MYSELF WITHOUT FEAR,
OBSERVING YOUR MOTIONLESS EYES,
NOTICING YOUR DISBELIEF EXPRESSION,
THE TONE OF YOUR VOICE VARIED
LEAVES ME WITH APPREHENSIVE DESIRE.

YET THIS ADDS TO MY FEAR,
MY THOUGHTS OF US AS A PAIR.
I'LL NOT DISCLOSE MY DESPAIR.
YOU WOULD WANT TO SWEAR.
I'LL NOT TELL OF MY DESIRE,
NEVER BEING A PAIR
GIVES ME SILENT TEARS.

TO KEEP FROM HAVING MY FEAR.
NEVER ABLE TO CALL YOU, DEAR,
JUST KEEP OUR FRIENDSHIP IN GEAR.
HOW PAINFUL THROUGH THE YEARS,
TO CONTINUE MY SILENT TEARS
WHILE CONTINUING WITH OUR CHEERS.

ca. 2001

MY HOURS OF REMINISCING

IN THESE HOURS OF REMINISCING,
FLASHBACKS VIVIDLY COMMENCING WITH YESTERDAYS
BEGINNINGS OF YESTERDAYS NOT OFTEN SPOKEN
YET LOCKED WITHIN THE HEART AND MIND
INCIDENTS OF YESTERDAYS OFTEN SUPPRESSED
INCIDENTS TOO PAINFUL TO HAVE SURFACED.

AH, BUT A FEW JOYS IMMERSION OCCURS
ALONG WITH MELANCHOLY TIMES
CONTRADICTION RAPIDLY FLOWS,
CONTINUING FROM ALL WALKS OF LIFE.
STRONG CENSURE FROM UNEXPECTED PLACES.
DENIAL FROM OUR GOVERNMENT AGENCIES,
CENSURE OF OUR CHURCH DENOMINATIONS,
OBJECTIONS FROM DIVERSE CULTURAL FAMILIES,
RENUNCIATION FROM MAGNITUDE OF INSTITUTIONS.

IN HUMAN EARLY STAGES OF DEVELOPMENT
ALL THESE OPPOSITIONS CAUSE MASS CONFUSION.
MANY END UP OVER COMPENSATORY TRAITS.
THIS CAN LEAD TO AN ENORMOUS DISASTER
CASES OF SEVERE CONSEQUENCES BEGINNING
IN EARLY STAGES OF OUR DEVELOPMENT.
THE VELOCITY OF THE DISSIMILARITY MAY
NEVER BE FULLY REALIZED, ANALYZED, OR DIAGNOSED.

LATER, THROUGH FORMATIVE EDUCATION,
ENLIGHTENMENT REVEALS CONTRADICTIONS
PRESENTED IN MANY BLATANT FORMS
THUS, CAUSING ISSUES TO BECOME CONFUSING.
WHAT TO BELIEVE, WHAT NOT TO BELIEVE
SEEKING CLARIFICATION, SEARCHING FOR TRUTHS,
ALL LEADING TO MORE LOGICALLY INCONGRUOUS,
MORE DENIALS, AND MORE MISTRUST.

NEVERTHELESS, THE SEARCH CONTINUES,
DISCOVERING CONTRADICTIONS ARE INTENTIONAL.
A MEANS OF KEEPING THE MASSES UNINFORMED.
A METHOD OF DIVIDING THE CONFUSED MASSES.
A METHOD CONQUERING, BECOMING VICTORIOUS
OVER MORAL AND EVIL POWERS.
CONTRADICTIONS THAT ARE DISTORTED,
ESTABLISHING IGNORANCE FOR GENERATIONS.

THE MANY YEARS OF EDUCATION
HAVE SOME WITH THE VARYING OPINIONS,
ASSUMING THEY KNOW THE TRUTHS,
SOME INSIGHTFUL ENOUGH TO REALIZE
THE MULTITUDINOUS CONTRADICTIONS,
WHILE SOME USE THEIR TRAINING, THEIR WIT
TO CONTINUE PERPETUATING CONTRADICTIONS
INCONSISTENCIES DUE TO LANGUAGE INTERPRETATIONS,
CAUSING CONTRADICTIONS AND MORE DENIALS.

THROUGH GOVERNMENTAL ASSIGNMENTS,
THROUGH THEIR EDUCATIONAL ENDEAVORS,
THROUGH THE VARIOUS RELIGIONS OFFERED,
THROUGH MASSES OF SOCIETAL ACTIVITIES,
THROUGH CONSIDERABLE CULTURAL DIVERSITIES
CONTRADICTIONS CONTINUE TO PREVAIL,
CAUSING ADDITIONAL DISCOMFORT
TO THE HEARTS AND MINDS.

THESE FLASHBACKS HUMBLE ONE.
YET IT ANGERS ONE
WHILE LEAVING ONE MELANCHOLY
REALITY OF ALL THE CONTRADICTIONS,
THE CULTURAL DISSIMILARITIES,
VARIANT DEGREES OF EDUCATIONAL KNOWLEDGE,
THE VARIOUS RELIGIOUS DIFFERENCES
HAVE CAUSED DISTINCT DIFFERENCES SINCE THE
BEGINNING OF MANKIND.

THUS, VARIOUS RELIGIOUS CONTRADICTIONS
VARY, DEPENDING ON THEIR DETERMINED PURPOSE.
MANY FOLLOWERS BECOME DISENCHANTED,
MANY WORSHIPERS LEAVE THEIR CHURCHES,
SOME PARISHIONERS CHANGE THEIR RELIGION,
WHILE THEY SEARCH FOR THE TRUTH.
SOME FOLLOWERS, UNABLE TO HANDLE INCONSISTENCY
THEIR NEW AWARENESS, SUBMIT TO VARIOUS
DEGREES AND FORMS OF DISOBEDIENCE.

REFLECTING ON YEARS DISOBEDIENCE HAS OCCURRED,
REFLECTIONS OF MANY CONTRADICTIONS ARE
ILLUMINATED IN MY DISTRESSED MIND.
FRUSTRATION CAUSING UNSETTLING EXPERIENCES
MOMENTS OF EXTREME BITTERNESS,
MOMENTS OF HEIGHTENED ANGER,
MOMENTS OF HATE AND MISTRUST,
MOMENTS OF DESIRED RETALIATIONS.

REFLECTING ON THESE DISOBEDIENCES PERPETRATED
SOMETIMES AGAINST THE GOVERNMENT,
SOMETIMES AGAINST OUR SOCIETY,
SOMETIMES AGAINST OUR FAMILY,
SOMETIMES AGAINST OUR FRIENDS,
AND EVEN SOMETIMES AGAINST SELF
GIVING IRRITANT TO MIND AND SOUL
IN MY HOURS OF REMINISCING.

ca. 2006

MY 9-11-01

THE TELEVISION ALREADY ON FOR VIEWING,
THE CLOCK WAS QUIETLY TICKING,
AS I CASUALLY LAY SINKING INTO SLEEP
AND THEN OUT OF SLEEP.
EYES OPENING TO SEE THE DESPICABLE ACT.
IS THE ORDEAL REAL OR A HORRIFYING DREAM?
SURELY, I MUST NOT BE AWAKE.
THIS ALL MUST BE IN MY DREAM.

REALITY INTERRUPTS MY CONSCIOUSNESS.
SUDDENLY, I SPRANG UP FROM MY BED.
WHAT IS THIS? HOW CAN THIS BE?
THE SHOCK WAS MUCH TOO GREAT.
HOW COULD THIS BE HAPPENING?
SO FAR AWAY TO COMPREHEND;
YET RIGHT BEFORE MY EYES,
OH, SO CLOSE ON 9-11-01.

ca. 2001

MY INQUISITION

YEARS OF INNOVATIVENESS LEAD TO MY INQUISITION.
HERE I SIT, ELBOWS RESTING UPON MY KNEES,
HEAD CUPPED IN THE MOISTURE OF MY HANDS.
I TIGHTLY CLOSE MY WEARY EYES.
I HEAR THE PULSATION SOUNDS OF THIS BODY.
TIME REVEALS READINESS MIGRATION,
PIERCING MY MIGHTY INNER RECESSES.
SLOWLY, IMMERSING INTO THE INNERMOST OF ME,
ENGULFING QUIETNESS AS I'M DESCENDING,
DESCENDING DEEPER AND DEEPER AND DEEPER.

IN THIS INCREDIBLE DARKNESS, THERE IS STILLNESS.
I LISTEN WITH ANXIETY TO MY ERUPTING INNARDS
IN THE CORRIDORS OF MY QUIVERING ORGANS.
THIS EMPRISE GRADUALLY BEGINS TO ILLUMINATE.
MY BREATHING BECOMES NOTICEABLE HALTINGLY.
MY SKIN URGENTLY DISCHARGES SWEAT RAPIDLY.
EXTRINSICALLY, MY ECTOMORPH IS DISSOLVED.
A BRIGHT BEAM INFILTRATES MY SPIRITUAL WORLD.
LIGHT REVEALS THE MAGNITUDE OF INTERNAL SELF.

I SEARCH THE VITAL PRINCIPLES OF MY EMBODIMENT.
THEORETICALLY, THE PREMISE IS THERE.
AMBIGUITIES UNFOLD OF THIS INNER INTERROGATION.
A DELUSION, CAUSING ME EMOTIONAL ANGUISH.
DYNAMICS OF MY PHYSIOLOGICAL BEING REVEALED.
THIS BROADENS MY EXTRASENSORY PERCEPTION.
PSYCHOLOGICALLY, MANIPULATION BECOMES VISIBLE.
THE SOCIOLOGICAL MYSTIQUE REFLECTS MY MILIEU,
HERE, AT THE DEPTH OF THIS INQUISITION,
PENETRATING THROUGH ALL OF THIS MASS,
THE INTROVERSION DISSECTING CONCLUDED.

IN CONCLUSION OF MY SELF-INVENTORY,
I AM PARAPSYCHOLOGICALLY ENLIGHTENED.
THE IMMORALITY OF MY BEING CONTINUES,
CLEARING MY PSYCHOGENESIS, MY SOCIABILITY,
INCLUDING MY IDEOLOGY AND SPIRITUAL THEOPATHY.
I AM BACK TO THE RUDIMENTS OF THE PHYSICAL ME,
REALIZING THE ANTHROPOCENTRIC OF MY EMBODIMENT.
THUS, I STRIVE FOR THE INTRINSIC ONENESS WITH THE UNIVERSE!

ca. 2001

MY TIME HAS COME

WE KNOW NOT WHEN OUR TRANSITION.
NOW MY TIME HAS COME.
I HAVE FILLED ALL MY REQUISITIONS
THAT LIFE PLACED BEFORE ME.
MANY OF MY DEEDS WITHOUT RECOGNITION
THAT WERE REQUIRED OF ME,
MANY PROFESSIONAL RESTRICTIONS
THAT WERE ENHANCING MY LIFE'S QUALITY,
MANY FORMAL AND INFORMAL CONTRIBUTIONS
THAT WERE EXPECTED OF ME,
MANY WONDERFUL ACTS OF JUBILATIONS
THAT WERE PART OF MY CELEBRATION.

NOW MY TIME HAS COME.
NO MORE UNAPPRECIATED OBLIGATIONS,
NO MORE SOCIETAL DEMANDS OR EXPECTATIONS,
NO MORE UNSPOKEN PAIN AND SUFFERING,
NO MORE EARTHLY REQUIREMENTS FOR ME.

NOW MY TIME HAS COME.
TIME TO SPEND RESTING AND REJOICING
FROM ALL MANKIND'S EARTHLY ENDEAVORS.
TIME TO BE AN ANGEL WITH THE FLOCK ON HIGH,
DRESSING IN THE PURE ANGELIC WHITE GOWN,
TIME TO JOIN WITH MY HEAVENLY CAREGIVER,
LEAVING MY PERSONAL LANGUISH BEHIND,
TIME TO SAY FAREWELL TO FAMILY AND FRIENDS,
AS I WILL PEACEFULLY AWAIT YOUR ARRIVAL,
MY TIME HAS COME!

APRIL 15, 2006

MY PART

IN TIMES OF DESPAIR,
LET ME STAND FOR RIGHTNESS
EVEN THOUGH WRONGS SURROUND.

IN TIMES OF UNCERTAINTY,
LET ME SET POSITIVE EXAMPLES
EVEN WHEN SOME ARE DAMAGING.

IN TIMES OF CHAOS,
LET ME GIVE WHAT I CAN
EVEN AS THOSE TAKE AT WILL.

IN TIMES OF POVERTY,
LET ME SUPPORT THOSE IN NEED
EVEN THOUGH OTHERS REFUSE.

IN TIMES OF DESTRUCTION,
LET ME GIVE THANKS FOR THIS DAY
EVEN AS SOME CONDEMN THIS DAY.

IN TIMES OF HATRED,
LET ME PRAY FOR MANKIND
EVEN WHILE THOSE ARE DESTROYING.

THEN, I HAVE FOLLOWED HIS TEACHINGS.
THEN, I WILL HAVE DONE MY PART.
THEN, I CAN SECURE PEACE OF MIND.

ca. 2001

MY SISTER, MY SISTER

MY SISTER, MY SISTER
WHAT HAVE YOU DONE?
SHE TRIES TO DO
ALL THINGS FOR EACH ONE.
IF IT WILL BE DONE
MY SISTER IS THE ONE,
WHATEVER IS TO BE DONE.

MY SISTER CAN'T BE BLAMED.
SHE OFFERS NO SHAME
ON HER, THEY LAY THEIR CLAIM.
NO MATTER WHETHER IN PAIN
IT'S ALWAYS THE SAME
MY SISTER IS THE ONE,
WHATEVER IS TO BE DONE.

MY SISTER WORKS DAY AND NIGHT,
SHE CONTINUES UNTIL IT'S RIGHT.
NO ASSIGNMENT FOR ANYONE,
NO CHORES FOR HER CHILDREN,
NO EXPECTATIONS FROM HER MATE.
MY SISTER IS THE ONE,
WHATEVER IS TO BE DONE.

MY SISTER WILL PREVAIL.
SHE WILL OVERCOME
JUST LEAVE IT TO HER
UNTIL IT'S ALL DONE
MY SISTER IS THE ONE,
WHATEVER IS TO BE DONE.

THAT'S MY SISTER, MY SISTER.

ca. 2002

NO ORDINARY MAN

BEGINNING OF HIS EMERGENCE UPON THE NATIONAL STAGE,
VISIONARY OF A MAN WITH DIVINE INTERVENTION,
THE INTROSPECT REVEALS HE IS TRULY NO ORDINARY MAN.
HIS MERE PRESENCE DEMANDS HYPNOTIC ATTENTION,
HIS DELIGHTFUL ELEGANT DASHING DEMEANOR,
HIS CHARMING GENUINE DISARMING PERSONALITY
LEAVE AMAZINGLY MENTAL ASTONISHMENT
REALLY, HE IS NO ORDINARY MAN.

OBSERVING HIS EXTRAORDINARY COMMAND
OF THE PROPER ENGLISH VOCABULARY,
OBSERVING HIS LOQUACIOUS DELIVERIES,
OBSERVING HIS UNFLAPPABLE, STEADFAST DETERMINATION,
THROUGHOUT HIS TWO YEARS OF CAMPAIGNING
GIVES TRUE REFLECTIVE REALIZATION THAT
CORRECTLY, HE IS NO ORDINARY MAN.

THE GREAT JOY CAUSES RAPTURE IN THE BODY.
THE PRIDE BRINGS INEXPLICABLE HAPPINESS.
UNCONTROLLABLE TEARS RELEASED SLOWLY STREAMING.
EMPHATICALLY CONCLUDE THAT
EARNESTLY, HE IS NO ORDINARY MAN.

WATCHING TWO MILLION FRAZZLED PEOPLE
PHYSICALLY LISTENING
TO THE OATH ADMINISTERED TO HIM,
WATCHING HIM BECOMING PRESIDENT!
IN RETROSPECT, NEVER CONTEMPLATED IN THIS LIFETIME;
WATCHING HIS HISTORICAL, PROFOUND ORATION TO THE WORLD
LEGITIMATELY, BY THIS NO ORDINARY MAN.

STROLLING BEFORE MILLIONS, DOWN THE AVENUE IN FRIGID
WEATHER AS HE MAKES HIS WAY TO THE WHITE HOUSE.
APPEARANCES AT THE NUMEROUS INAUGURAL BALLS,
STARING DIRECTLY INTO THE TELEVISION,
HE HAS TRIUMPHANTLY COME FORTH,
HE IS AN ABSOLUTE PROPHET OF DIVINE POWERS.
PRAISE TO THIS RENOWNED WORLD LEADER
SIGNIFY ASSUREDLY HE IS NO ORDINARY MAN.

KNOWN TO THE WORLD AS
PRESIDENT BARACK HUSSEIN OBAMA!
FORTY-FOURTH PRESIDENT OF THE UNITED STATES OF AMERICA!

JANUARY 2009

ONE NEVER KNOWS

MOTHER, NOW AS YOU LIE IN PEACE,
I RECALL THROUGH THE YEARS
I HEARD YOU SAY,
"ONE NEVER KNOWS"

NEVER KNOWING WHAT DAWN WOULD HOLD
WHAT ANOTHER NIGHT WOULD FOLD.
I'VE REFLECTED ON THE PASSING TIMES,
EVENTS THAT OCCURRED
ON THE GOOD TIMES
OR THE BAD TIMES TOO.
"ONE NEVER KNOWS"

I'VE PEERED THROUGH MISTY EYES.
THE SCENTED AIR RUSHED THROUGH MY NOSTRILS.
I'VE REALIZED MOISTURE IN MY PALMS.
THE BLOOD RAPIDLY PUSHED THROUGH MY VEINS
I'VE GUARDED MY TREMBLING BODY.
THE STURDIED OF MY WEAK STANCE.
I'VE IGNORED THE ELEVATION OF MY TEMPERATURE.
THE RESULT OF MY ANXIETY
AS I POSITIONED AT BEDSIDE.
"ONE NEVER KNOWS"

I'VE WATCHED FROWNING UPON YOUR FOREHEAD.
THE PUMPING OF YOUR FEEDING TUBE.
I'VE NOTICED YOUR BODY SLIGHTLY MOVING
EVEN AWARE OF YOUR CHEST HEAVING.
I'VE OBSERVED YOUR LIPS QUIVERING,
AT TIMES, YOUR EYES SLIGHTLY AJAR.
I'VE FELT THE GRASP OF YOUR HANDS.
YES, EVEN THEIR COLDNESS TOO.
"ONE NEVER KNOWS"

SILENTLY, I HAVE PRAYED,
"OH, MY LORD, I AM WATCHING,
I AM WITNESSING THIS ORDEAL.
BESTOW TENDER MERCY UPON YOU,
YOU HAVE PAID YOUR DUES IN FULL.
I ASKED, DEAR HEAVENLY FATHER,
HOW MUCH LONGER
MUST YOU HAVE TO ENDURE?"
"ONE NEVER KNOWS"

NOW, STILLNESS OF LIFE SURROUNDS ME.
GRASPING MY FLEETING THOUGHTS,
REASSURING MYSELF OF THIS TRANSITION,
NOW THAT YOUR LIFE HAS GONE.
AS YOU DEPART FROM YOUR FAMILY,
AS YOU LEAVE YOUR LOVED ONES,
DARKNESS FILLS THIS AWESOME GLOOM.
"ONE NEVER KNOWS"

YOUR PEACEFULNESS HAS ARRIVED.
GOD HAS TAKEN YOU FROM US,
FROM YOUR EXCRUCIATING PAIN.
FOR HE HAS DELIVERED YOU
FROM YOUR TREMENDOUS SUFFERING.
YOUR SLUMBER TIME HAS FINALLY COME.
HE HAS BROUGHT YOU HOME.
MOTHER, "I NOW KNOW!"

YES, ETHEL, JAMES, HUSTON, SAMUEL,
CURTIS, MARILYN, AND ROSCOE, NOW KNOW TOO,
ALONG WITH OUR RELATIVES AND YOUR FRIENDS.
YOU ARE IN GOD'S TENDER CARE!
FAREWELL, REST AS YOU SO DESERVINGLY NEED.

ca. 2003

OUR COURAGEOUS PRINCE

LADIES AND GENTLEMEN, FRIEND OR FOE,
LET SOCIETY KNOW THAT SHAWN,
OUR COURAGEOUS PRINCE,
SUFFERED A TREMENDOUS BLOW.
IT COULD HAVE TAKEN ITS TOLL.

WHEN REQUIRED TO GO SLOW,
COULD HAVE SANK EXTREMELY LOW,
COULD HAVE EVEN ENDED HIS FLOW,
SHOWED HE WITHSTOOD THE BLOW,
HE CONTINUES IN HIS GLOW.

WHILE THERE WERE CONCERNS,
HE HAS SHOWN HIS TENACITY.
OUR COURAGEOUS PRINCE
ELIMINATED OUR QUESTIONS.
WHEN THERE WAS SADNESS
RATHER THAN MADNESS,
HE GAVE US HAPPINESS.

OUR COURAGEOUS PRINCE
HAS CAUSED MANKIND TO YIELD,
HEAR YEA, HEAR YEA!
THE ACCOLADES ARE RAISED.
LIFT YOUR VOICES IN PRAISE!

TO ALL, LET IT BE KNOWN,
OUR GALLANT SHAWN, WE BOW.
AFTER SUFFERING A TREMENDOUS BLOW,
HIS DETERMINATION CONTINUES TO GROW.
SHOWN US, HE WILL CONTINUE HIS FLOW.

ca. 2001

OUR QUEEN MOTHER

IN OUR WORLD OF TODAY,
THERE ARE QUEENLIKE MOTHERS.
SOME ARE MAJESTIC,
SOME ARE REGAL,
NONE RADIATES AS OUR QUEEN MOTHER.

THERE IS OUR QUEEN MOTHER,
AND THERE IS NO OTHER.
YOU WILL SOON REALIZE
HER SOVEREIGN SECOND TO NONE.

THERE ARE OTHER QUEEN MOTHERS,
SOME PORTRAY SUPERIOR QUALITIES,
SOME HAVING EMINENT PROJECTIONS,
SOME EXHIBIT SUPREME AUTHORITIES.

BEFORE HER, THERE WAS NO OTHER
YOU WILL FIND YOURSELF IN THE
PRESENCE OF AN IMPORTANT PERSON,
NO MATTER, YOU'RE NO BOTHER.

HER PROMINENCE PERSONA IS POWERFUL,
REIGNS SOVEREIGNLY OVER HER DOMAIN
THUS, YOU WILL UNDERSTAND
OUR VISCOUNTESS EXHIBITS TENACITY.
AFTER ALL, THERE IS NO OTHER,
SHE IS OUR QUEEN MOTHER.

ca. 2003

PRANCERS

TAKE NOTE, SOCIETY IS FULL OF PRANCERS.
PRANCERS ARE OBSERVED IN MANY SITUATIONS
AND RESULT OF NUMEROUS CIRCUMSTANCES.
FATHERS ARE PRANCERS AWAITING ARRIVAL OF BIRTH.
MINISTERS ARE PRANCERS DELIVERING THEIR SERMONS.
COACHES PRANCE ALONG SIDELINES AT ATHLETIC GAMES.
ATHLETES ARE PRANCERS WHILE WAITING FOR PRACTICE.
BOXERS ARE PRANCERS IN THE RING DURING THEIR FIGHTS.
TEACHERS ARE PRANCERS WHILE PRESENTING LECTURES.
LADIES OF THE EVENING PRANCE UP AND DOWN STREETS.
PEOPLE AGITATED ARE PRANCERS FOR VARIOUS CAUSES.

SOME PRANCERS ARE UNABLE TO STAND STILL,
INDECISIVENESS CAUSES SOME TO BE PRANCERS.
MANAGEMENT OFTEN PRANCES WHILE OBSERVING STAFF.
ATTORNEYS PRANCE WHILE PRESENTING THEIR CASES.
SALES PEOPLE ARE PRANCERS WHILE SELLING MERCHANDISE.
GUARDSMEN ARE PRANCERS WHILE KEEPING THEIR WATCH.
WAITERS ARE PRANCERS WHILE WAITING ON CUSTOMERS.
PARKING ATTENDANTS DO A LOT OF PRANCING PARKING CARS.
ENTERTAINERS OFTEN ARE PRANCERS WHILE PERFORMING.
EVIDENTLY, ALL HAVE BEEN PRANCERS,
AT ONE TIME OR ON ONE OCCASION
SO, HOORAY FOR PRANCERS!

ca. 2006

PRAY

OH, HUMAN BEINGS OF THE WORLD, PRAY
ALL CITIZENS OF OUR NATIONS, PRAY
TO THE RACES OF EVERY COUNTRY, PRAY
ALL NATIONALITIES OF OUR UNIVERSE, PRAY
RAISE YOUR VOICES IN UNISON AND PRAY
LET EACH OF US IN OUR OWN WAY PRAY
ASK FOR A BETTER TOMORROW AS WE PRAY
GIVE US HOPE, GIVE US PEACE, WE PRAY
PROVIDE LOVE AND UNDERSTANDING, WE PRAY
LET IT BE HEARD LOUD AND CLEAR, PRAY
FOR ALL OF MANKIND, PRAY!
PRAY!

ca. 2004

PRINCE CHARMING

HE QUIETLY ARRIVED AT THE ENTRANCE,
APPEARING A TRIFLE SHY,
SOMEWHAT A LITTLE HESITANT,
HE WAS INTRODUCED AS "TONY"
AS HE WAS WARMLY GREETED
SEEMED TO RELAX AMONG THE GUEST.

IN OBSERVANCE OF TONY,
YET HE'S ONLY A YOUNG LAD.
DEMONSTRATING A DEGREE OF MATURITY,
HE PRESENTED HIMSELF WITH GRACE.
HIS HANDSOME LOOKS WERE STRIKING.
HE PROJECTED A SMILE THAT WAS DISARMING,
HIS QUIET DEMEANOR GAVE A DELIGHTFUL PRESENCE.
THIS LED ME TO DECLARE HIM, "PRINCE CHARMING"

THE YOUNG LADIES PRESENT
DEMONSTRATED A DEGREE OF EXCITEMENT
EVEN THOUGH SEVERAL YEARS HIS SENIOR,
HIS YOUNG AGE DIDN'T SEEM TO MATTER
INSTANTLY, IT BECAME APPARENT
HE WAS IN FOR A HEAVY PURSUIT.
SOMEHOW, "PRINCE CHARMING"
WILL HAVE TO LEARN
HOW TO HANDLE MANY PURSUITS.
WITNESSING HIS MODE OF ACTION
IT LED TO MY CONFIDENCE,
"PRINCE CHARMING" WILL.

ca. 2002

PRINCE DANIEL

PRINCE DANIEL, KNOWN AS THE NUMBER ONE,
STANDS READY TO TAKE ON EVERY ONE.
THOSE DETERMINED THEY KNEW BEST,
THOSE HAD MANIPULATED HIS TIME,
THOSE OFFERED HIM THEIR PLANS,
THOSE HAD EXHIBITED DESIRABLE ROLES,
THOSE PROVIDED THEIR EXCELLENT IDEAS,
THOSE INSISTED ON HIS SUITABLE GOALS,
ALL FOR HIS FUTURE ENDEAVORS,
THEY INCREDIBLY CAME UP SHORT IN THE END.

PRINCE DANIEL RELEASED FROM THEIR INFLUENCE.
MANY WEREN'T READY TO RELINQUISH THEIR GRASP,
READYING TO MOVE HIS LIFE FORWARD,
NOW HE HAS COME FULL CIRCLE.
HE PLANS TO ESTABLISH NEW GOALS.
THERE WILL BE NO LOOKING BACKWARD.
HE ASSUREDLY WILL STAND HIS GROUND,
CONTINUING TO EMBARK ON NEW PLANS.
PRINCE DANIEL PLANS TO MAKE UP LOST TIME.
HE PLANS TO CONTINUE BEING NUMBER ONE.

ca. 2004

PRINCESS BRANDI

TIMES I HAVE SEEN HER,
TIMES I HAVE OBSERVED HER,
TIMES I HAVE SPOKEN WITH HER,
QUALITIES OF A PRINCESS NOTICED.

HER PERSONALITY INDICATES NO HARM,
SHE RADIATES WITH CHARM,
CONFIDENCE PROVIDES A QUIET CALM.
IT WOULD BE ONLY TIME
WHEN OTHERS WOULD REALIZE
SHE'D BECOME PRINCESS BRANDI.

SHE ELEGANTLY GLIDES THROUGH THE CROWD.
HER GAIT WITH SUCH GRACE,
ADORNED IN A GOWN OF EXQUISITE BEAUTY,
WEARING HER CROWN OF GLITTER.

PRINCESS BRANDI, NOW EVERYONE KNOWS
WHAT I HAVE KNOWN,
SHE IS PRINCESS BRANDI IN THEIR TOWN!

ca. 2000

QUESTIONING LOVE

IF THIS EMOTIONAL DESIRE PERSISTS,
IF THIS PALPITATION CONTINUES IN MY HEART,
IF THESE ENDLESS NIGHTS CONTINUE,
IF THE WAITING BY THE PHONE PREVAILS,
IF THE DAYDREAMING PURSUES,
IF THE REMINISCENCE OF YOU RETAINED,
THEN, THIS MUST BE LOVE.

IF YOU ALLOW MY DREAMS FULFILLED,
IF YOU LET ME REMAIN ME,
IF YOU ARE WILLING TO SHARE,
IF YOU ARE UNWILLING TO TAKE ALL,
IF YOU GIVE UNCONVENTIONAL TRUST,
IF YOU ACCEPT ME AS YOUR EQUAL,
IF YOU BELIEVE IN ME
AS I BELIEVE IN YOU,
THEN, THIS MUST BE LOVE.

ca. 2003

RAYMOND, MY FRIEND

TO LEARN OF YOUR DEMISE, MY FRIEND,
THE AWARENESS THERE IS NO MORE RAYMOND
CAUSED A SOLEMN MOOD OF DOOM AND GLOOM,
CAUSING AN EMOTIONAL, DESOLATE, AND DREARY TIME.
MOMENTARILY, A FEELING ENGULFED IN DARKNESS
WHILE IN MY STATE OF DIRE GRIEF AND SADNESS.
IT GAVE ME THE OPPORTUNITY TO REMINISCE.
RECALLING THE YEARS OF OUR FRIENDSHIP,
RECOUNTING YOUR MANY BESTOWED ACCOLADES,
YOUR MANY, MANY SUPERB ACCOMPLISHMENTS,
YES, ALSO, YOUR TRIALS AND TRIBULATIONS TOO.
RAYMOND, REMEMBERING THE MAN MANY LOVED.

THE COUNTLESS YEARS OF OUR LOYAL FRIENDSHIP
PROVIDE SOLACE, NOW THAT YOU'VE DEPARTED.
FURTHER REMEMBRANCE OF YOU, MY FRIEND,
SILENTLY LEAVES A STATE OF DISMAL REMORSE.
WHEN GOD CALLED YOU TO USE YOUR ATTRIBUTES,
SOFTLY AND GENTLY SURRENDERED YOUR LIFE.
YOU MY FRIEND, A MAN OF GENUINE DEPTH,
YOU MY FRIEND, A MAN OF GREAT HUMILITY,
YOU MY FRIEND, A MAN OF SINCERE HONESTY,
YOU MY FRIEND, A MAN OF TREMENDOUS LOYALTY,
YOU MY FRIEND, A MAN OF GREAT UNDERSTANDING,
YOU MY FRIEND, A MAN WITH OUTSTANDING TALENT.

SO, GOOD-BYE MY FRIEND, MAY YOU REST IN PEACE.
NO MORE DISILLUSION, NO MORE PAIN OR SUFFERING,
CONTINUE TO WALK AS PROUDLY AMONG THE ANGELS,
WITH CONFIDENCE, WITH DIGNITY, AND WITH PRIDE,
AS YOU WALKED AMONG YOUR FELLOW MEN HERE.

OCTOBER 2004

RECESSES OF MY MIND

IN THE DEEP, DEEP, DEEP
RECESSES OF MY DISTORTED FRAGILE MIND
ARE MANY, REPEATEDLY TROUBLING ISSUES:
THERE ARE FREQUENT COMPLEX ANXIETIES,
THERE ARE NUMEROUS AWESOME OPINIONS,
THERE ARE MULTIPLE QUESTIONABLE THEORIES
ALL IN THE RECESSES OF MY MIND.
THE REPREHEND HARROW NO ONE SHOULD PROCESS.
THE MYSTERIES OF CRAVING RELENTLESS DESIRES.
THE HEINOUS FRUSTRATIONS LOOM HEAVILY
IN THE RECESSES OF MY MIND.
ATTEMPT TO CONCEAL THE TRUE AGONY,
ATTEMPT TO SUBMERGE THESE THOUGHTS,
ATTEMPT TO SUPPRESS THE DESPERATION,
IN THE RECESSES OF MY MIND.
DEEP, DEEP, DEEP IN THE
RECESSES OF MY DISTORTED, FRAGILE MIND.

ca. 2006

REFLECTIONS OF MOTHER DEAR

TODAY, TORN WITH GRIEF,
    I SOLEMNLY REFLECT ON YOU,
        MOTHER, DEAR.

IN THOSE DAYS,
    AS A CHILD, YOU WERE THERE
        TO SEE THAT I HAD THE BEST YOU COULD
        GIVE,
        MOTHER, DEAR.

WHEN I DID NOT ALWAYS GIVE MY ALL,
    WHEN I DID NOT DO MY BEST,
        YOU SHOWED PATIENCE AND
        UNDERSTANDING,
        MOTHER, DEAR.

MY ADOLESCENT YEARS
    WERE FILLED WITH ONE ISSUE AND THEN ANOTHER.
    YET YOU SHOWED COMPASSION AND
        YOU GAVE ME PROTECTION,
        MOTHER, DEAR.

BUT MOST OF ALL, MY MINDFUL AND TENDER
    REFLECTION OF YOU IS YOUR UNSELFISHNESS,
        AND THE GENUINE LOVE YOU EXHIBITED,
        MOTHER, DEAR.

AS A YOUNG MAN
YOU GAVE ME ASSISTANCE,
YOU DEFENDED ME WHEN I WAS WRONGED,
YOU SUPPORTED ME, NO MATTER
WHAT!
THE TRUE LOVE OF A
DEDICATED
MOTHER, DEAR.

SITTING HERE WITH A HEAVY HEART AND REFLECTING ON
ALL YOUR CARING,
ALL YOUR LOVING,
ALL YOUR PROTECTIVENESS, AND
ALL THE TENDERNESS YOU GAVE.
MOTHER, DEAR.

YOU ALWAYS WANTED THE BEST FOR ME, AND
YOU ALWAYS DEMANDED THE VERY BEST FOR ME,
MOTHER, DEAR.

THE GENEROSITY YOU SHARED WITH OTHERS,
THE CONCERN AND THOUGHTFULNESS TOWARD
FAMILY AND FRIENDS WILL ALWAYS BE
WITH ME,
MOTHER, DEAR.

THEN, TIME CAME AROUND FOR MY GIVING TO YOU,
AND MY SACRIFICING FOR YOU,
MOTHER, DEAR.

LORD KNOWS I DID THE BEST I COULD,
FOR AS LONG AS I WAS ABLE,
EVEN THOUGH THE BURDEN WAS HEAVY,
MOTHER, DEAR.

NOW, AS YOU REST IN GOD'S GENTLE ARMS,
    HE WILL GIVE YOU ALL THE LOVE, AND
        HE WILL GIVE YOU THE CARE
            YOU SO RIGHTLY DESERVE,
                MOTHER, DEAR.

SO, WHILE IN MY AGONY AND WHILE REFLECTING,
    I HUMBLY PRAY THAT YOU ARE NOW AT PEACE,
        YOU FOUGHT LIFE'S GALLANT BATTLE,
            MOTHER, DEAR.

YOU SHOWED ME HOW TO LIVE LIFE TO ITS FULLEST.
    YOU DEMONSTRATED HOW TO QUIETLY END
        THE STRUGGLE WHEN GOD CALLED YOU
        HOME,
            MOTHER, DEAR.

HERE I AM NOW, LIMPED AND TREMBLING,
    YET TRYING TO APPEAR REGAL AND STRONG;
        SO . . . "G O O D—B Y E" . . .
            SLEEP . . . SLEEP ON . . .
            SLEEP IN PEACE,
            M O T H E R, D E A R.

            YOUR LOVING SON,

            BRUCE VON RAY
            JOYNER SR.

                ca. 1999

RICH WHITE WOMENS' AUDACITY

RICH WHITE WOMEN'S AUDACITY IS AMAZING.
THEIR NERVES ARE TOTALLY MYSTIFYING.
THEIR PRESUMPTUOUSNESS IS FLAUNTING.
THEIR QUALIFICATIONS ARE OF QUESTIONING.
THEIR CONDESCENDING ATTITUDE'S APPALLING.
AFTER ALL:
THEY ARE RICH; THEY ARE WHITE; THEY ARE WOMEN.

THEY DON'T NEED ANY EXPERIENCE.
THEY DON'T NEED ANY PREREQUISITES.
THEY DON'T NEED TO POSSESS INTEGRITY.
THEY DON'T HAVE TO ABIDE BY THE LAWS.
AFTER ALL:
THEY ARE RICH; THEY ARE WHITE; THEY ARE WOMEN.

THEIR SUPPOSITION IS THAT THE PUBLIC ARE NITWITS,
THE CITIZENS WILL BUY THEIR INSOLENT ADVERTISING,
THE PEOPLE WILL SURELY ACCEPT THEIR BRAZEN ATTACKS,
THEY CAN SATURATE THE MEDIA WITH CATCHY SOUND BITES.
AFTER ALL:
THEY ARE RICH; THEY ARE WHITE; THEY ARE WOMEN.

NEVER MIND THEIR DEDICATION IN PROVIDING JOBS,
NEVER MIND THEIR GENUINENESS TOWARD EDUCATION,
NEVER MIND THEIR COMMITMENTS TO THE ENVIRONMENT,
NEVER MIND THEIR HONEST CONCERNS ABOUT IMMIGRATION,
AFTER ALL:
THEY ARE RICH; THEY ARE WHITE; THEY ARE WOMEN.

THESE WOMEN, CARLY, MEG, AND EVEN SARAH
ARE TOTALLY INTERESTED IN ONLY THEIR GAINS.
THESE POSITIONS DON'T PAY THAT MUCH FOR THEM,
ONLY HIPPOCRATIC PRETENSE AS THEY EXPLOIT THE PEOPLE.
THE PUBLIC ARE TOTALLY UNAWARE OF THEIR CONNIVING EFFORTS.
AFTER ALL:
THEY ARE RICH; THEY ARE WHITE; THEY ARE WOMEN.

THEIR MILLIONS COULD MORE EFFECTIVELY BE SPENT
OFFERING MUCH-NEEDED FUNDS IN FEEDING THE HUNGRY,
PROVIDING FANTASTIC SHELTER FOR THE MANY HOMELESS,
AND ESTABLISHING ELABORATE EDUCATIONAL FUNDS
FOR CHILDREN.
AFTER ALL:
THEY ARE RICH; THEY ARE WHITE; THEY ARE WOMEN.

THEY ARE COGNIZANT THAT IT IS NOT A CORPORATION.
CALIFORNIA DOES HAVE A CHECK AND BALANCE SYSTEM.
THEY MUST ABIDE BY THE STATE'S CONSTITUTIONAL RIGHTS.
THEY MUST FOLLOW LEGISLATIONS,
PREVENTING CALLOUS INVENTIONS.
EVEN THOUGH:
THEY ARE RICH; THEY ARE WHITE; THEY ARE WOMEN.

THIS PERSONA IS INDICATIVE OF RICH, WHITE WOMEN.
THEY ARE TRULY RICH, WHITE WOMEN WITH AUDACITY.
THEY ARE SELF-SERVING, ARROGANT,
AND EGOCENTRIC WHITE WOMEN.
THEY ARE WITHOUT ANY CONSCIENCE SENSE OF MORAL
OBLIGATION.

ca. 2010

SERGEANT/GENERAL SONNY PATTEN

A MILITARY CAREER OF THIRTY-PLUS YEARS OVERALL,
HE STANDS ABOUT FIVE AND A HALF FEET TALL.
GUESS HIS WEIGHT, YOU'RE ON THE BALL.
SOME CALL HIM SERGEANT/GENERAL SONNY PATTEN,
WHILE OTHERS DON'T HIM CALL AT ALL.
THE COMMUNICATIVENESS OF HIS TONE
YOU WILL THINK HE'S NOT ALONE.
OBSERVE HIS EXHIBITED PHYSICAL ACTIONS
REALIZE YOU'RE CONFRONTING A MILITARY MAN.

NOW BE PREPARED FOR A FUSS.
HE WILL HAVE TO SAY OR BUSS,
IN HIS PRESENCE LONG ENOUGH
YOU'LL FIND HE'S NOT ROUGH,
THERE WILL BE NO HARM.
HE WILL DAZZLE YOU WITH CHARM,
ATTEMPTING TO HOLD YOU IN HIS PALM.

THERE ARE ISSUES HE HANDLES WITH CALM.
THERE ARE CONCERNS THAT GIVES HIM ALARM.
YES, THAT IS SERGEANT/GENERAL SONNY PATTEN,
HIS VOICE OFTEN APPEARS ON EDGE
EVEN WHEN NOT PRESENTING A PLEDGE.

ca. 2003

SELFISHNESS

SOCIETY IS MAD WITH SELFISHNESS
UNLESS THERE'S SOMETHING FOR THEM.
NO MATTER YOUR NEEDS,
THEY DON'T CARE.

SOUND OUT ABOUT YOUR SHORTCOMINGS,
NO ONE WILL LISTEN.
PRESENT SOMETHING OF THEIR INTEREST,
YOU GET THEIR ATTENTION.

YOUR ISSUES GO UNATTENDED,
NO ONE CARES.
YOUR IDEAS OFTEN IGNORED,
NO ONE CARES.
LIVES ARE JEOPARDIZED AND RUINED,
NO ONE CARES.

HEALTH CONDITIONS INATTENTIVE,
NO ONE CARES.
EDUCATIONAL OPPORTUNITIES DENIED,
NO ONE CARES.
GANGS ALLOWED TO RUN AMOCK,
NO ONE CARES.

IF IT DOESN'T HELP THEM,
NO ONE CARES.
THE DEMIGODS' ONLY INTEREST,
IS FOR THEIR BENEFITS,
CAUSING MANY TO BE DESTROYED
ALL DUE TO THEIR SELFISHNESS.

ca. 2003

SHADES OF CLOUDS

PEERING OUT AT THE SHADES OF CLOUDS,
NOTICING THEIR VARIOUS SHADES,
OBSERVING THE DIFFERENT CLOUD FORMS,
WATCHING AS THEY GRADUALLY FLOWED,
WATCHING AS THEY SLOWLY EXPANDED,
COVERING THE BRIGHT BLUE SKY.
I ASK MYSELF, WHY?

PEERING AT THE HUES OF TREE LEAVES
STANDING BEFORE THE SHADES OF CLOUDS,
NOTICING THE DIFFERENT COLOR OF LEAVES
WATCHING THE VARIOUS CLOUD FORMS,
AS THEY SILENTLY, PASSIVELY FLOATED BY
WHILE COVERING THE BRIGHT BLUE SKY.
I ASK MYSELF, WHY?

PEERING AT THE VARIOUS BIRDS
FLYING BEFORE THE SHADES OF CLOUDS,
OBSERVING THEM LIGHT GRACEFULLY
UPON ONE TREE AND THEN ANOTHER,
WHILE NOTICING THE DELICATE
SHIFTING SHADES OF CLOUDS
COVERING THE BRIGHT BLUE SKY.
I ASK MYSELF, WHY?

ca. 2004

S H O U T

AFTER A NIGHT OF EFFERVESCENT DELIGHT
MAKES ME WANT TO S H O U T.

IT HAS BEEN INVIGORATING; FILLING ME WITHIN
MAKES ME WANT TO S H O U T.

ANOTHER DAY OF MAGNIFICENT BEAUTY
MAKES ME WANT TO S H O U T.

THE AWARENESS OF ALL THE SIGHTS
MAKES ME WANT TO S H O U T.

NOTING ALL GOD'S GREAT CREATIONS
MAKES ME WANT TO S H O U T.

AWAKEN TO THE DAWN OF ANOTHER DAY
MAKES ME WANT TO S H O U T.

S H O U T FOR ALL THE JOY THAT FILLS ME.
S H O U T!

ca. 2004

SIR BRUCE

UPON THE PEDESTAL STANDS SIR BRUCE.
OUR VISCOUNT ON DISPLAY.
POSSESSES AN ACQUISITION OF DECORATIONS,
EXHIBITS AN ASSORTMENT OF EXPRESSIONS:
A MAN ADMIRINGLY AND ATTENTIVELY,
A MAN COMPASSIONATE AND SENSITIVE,
A MAN OF CONCILIATORY AND CORDIALITY,
A MAN COOPERATIVE AND SUPPORTIVE.

SIR BRUCE, OUR VISCOUNT ON DISPLAY.
A MAN OF ENERGETIC PROPULSION,
A MAN OF ESSENTIAL COMBINATIONS:
A MAN CAPABLE OF PROVIDING A FUNCTION,
A MAN AMENABLE TO INTRODUCING A SOLUTION,
A MAN ATTEMPTS TO AVOIDS ANY INDIGNATION,
A MAN SHARES HIS OPINIONS AND POSITION,
A MAN EXCLUDES CONFLICTS OR FRICTION.

SIR BRUCE, OUR VISCOUNT ON DISPLAY.
HE PRESENTS YOU AN ARRAY OF DECISIONS:
DIMINISHES RESERVATIONS, PRESENTS RESOLUTIONS,
ENTERTAINS EXCEPTIONS INSTEAD OF REJECTIONS,
OFFERS DISCOURSE OF OPERABLE DECLARATIONS,
EAGER TO ANNOUNCE HIS PREDICTIONS,
FOLLOWS HIS INTROSPECTION CONVICTIONS.

SIR BRUCE, OUR VISCOUNT ON DISPLAY.
HIS PROVISION HAS NO INTROVERSION.
ADVISES INCLUSION RATHER THAN EXCLUSION,
PREFERS PROGRESSION RATHER THAN AGGRESSION,
HIS MISSION, BARGAIN CONCESSIONS,
BUT, HE DOESN'T HOLD ANY ILLUSIONS,
REALIZES HE CAN'T LIVE UNDER DELUSIONS,
INVITES ALL TO ACCEPT HIS CONCLUSIONS,
A NOBLEMAN OF GENUINE HONOR AND RESPECT.
THIS IS SIR BRUCE,
OUR VISCOUNT ON DISPLAY.

ca. 2001

SIR DORIAN FRANK

IN THE SUPREME PRESENCE OF SIR FRANK,
HE WILL MESMERIZE YOU WITH HIS ATTITUDE,
NOT KNOWING THE DEGREE OF HIS SOLICITUDE.

SIR FRANK APPEARS CONSTANTLY ON THE MOVE,
UNAWARE WHETHER HE KNOWS HIS OWN LATITUDE,
OFTEN APPEARING AS A MASTERFUL MAN IN CONTROL,
NO MATTER WHAT DEEDS REVEAL HIS MULTITUDES.

SIR FRANK WILL FITTINGLY GRANT YOU AN AUDIENCE.
HIS GESTURES OVERWHELM YOU WITH GREAT GRATITUDE.
HE AMAZINGLY CAN DEMAND YOUR UNDIVIDED ATTENTION.
HIS WISE REMARKS ARE NEVER MERELY A PLATITUDE.
YET, OFTEN, BRILLIANTLY LEAVING ONE WONDERING
WHETHER HIS SUBJECTS EVER FEEL IN HIS SERVITUDE.

SIR FRANK DEMONSTRATES POWER AND FORTITUDE.
IT DOES NOT MATTER THE GRAVITY OF THE MAGNITUDE.
ONE WILL TRAVEL FOR HIM TO ANY LONGITUDE,
ALL WITHOUT REVEALING THEIR SOLITUDE
TO SIR DORIAN FRANK!

ca. 2005

SONGS

LISTENING TO SONGS GIVES GREAT JOY.
SOME SONGS LEAVE YOU SAD
EVEN SONGS CAUSE YOU TO SHED A TEAR.
SONGS THAT FILL YOU WITH EXUBERANCE.
SONGS THAT PUT YOU IN A MELANCHOLY WAY.
SONGS THAT PRESENT GREAT PAIN.
SONGS THAT BRING FORTH PAST DREAMS.
SONGS THAT LIFT YOU, GIVING HOPE.
SONGS OF PEACE AND TRANQUILLITY.
SONGS THAT OFFER PRAISE TO MANKIND.
SONGS, YES, SONGS FOR ALL KIND.

ca. 2004

THANKSGIVING TIME

AGAIN, ANOTHER THANKSGIVING IS HERE.
WE GIVE THANKS
FOR OUR MANY BLESSINGS,
THIS THANKSGIVING TIME IS HERE.

OUR FAMILIES AND OUR FRIENDS,
WE HOLD THEM TO BE DEAR.
THEY'VE COME FROM FAR,
THEY'VE COME FROM NEAR.

SOME, PERHAPS, TRAVELED IN FEAR.
AT THESE TROUBLED TIMES,
STILL, THEY HAVE APPEARED
AT THIS THANKSGIVING TIME.

WE REACH OUT AND SHARE,
OUR VOICES RAISED IN PRAISE.
WE OFFER OUR BLESSINGS FOR ALL.
WE PRAY, "MAY WE SEE ANOTHER YEAR?"

A TIME, WHEN WE CAN ONCE AGAIN
BE WITH FAMILIES AND WITH FRIENDS,
WITH GOOD FOOD AND GOOD WINE
TO CELEBRATE THANKSGIVING TIME.

ca. 2001

THE CELEBRATION OF LIFE AND DEATH

CELEBRATION OF LIFE ALWAYS APPEARS BRIGHT.
CELEBRATED TIME AND TIME AGAIN IN THE LIGHT.
CELEBRATION AROUSED ENORMOUS DELIGHT,
EVEN CELEBRATED TO GREAT HEIGHTS.
CELEBRATED TO AND FRO IN MANY FLIGHTS.
YET NOT KNOWING
WHEN DEATH WOULD END MY PLIGHT.

NOW, MY CELEBRATION IS NO LONGER BRIGHT.
REALITY OF MY CELEBRATION
HAS DIMMED MY LIGHT.
TIME HAS CEASED MY DELIGHT.
DEATH IS DESCENDING MY HEIGHT.
THERE WILL BE NO MORE FLIGHTS.
FOUGHT, YES, I'VE FOUGHT MY PLIGHT.

THERE WILL BE NO PITY PARTY HERE.
CELEBRATE YOU . . . AND YOU DON'T SLIGHT.
YES, MY LOVE,
CELEBRATE . . . OUR LIFE HAS BEEN TIGHT.

CELEBRATE, LIFE ENDS, NO MORE FRIGHT.
CELEBRATE, NOW DEATH COMES.
CELEBRATE . . .
CELEBRATE!
CEL-E-BRATE!

ca. 1999

THE FALLING SNOW

SITTING BY THE WINDOW,
WATCHING THE WONDERS
OF THE SILENT, CASCADING SNOW.

OBSERVING THE FALLING SNOW
STIRRING AT GOD'S GREAT SHOW,
WATCHING AS IT MAGICALLY AND
FRAGILELY BLOWS TO AND FRO.

EVERYTHING BECOMES GRACEFULLY SLOW.
DEEPER AND DEEPER IT GROWS.
NO ONE IS WILLING TO BLOW,
CAUSING MANKIND TO LIMIT ITS CROW.

DAYS AS WELL AS NIGHTS,
OUR OFFICIALS ARE ON SNOW PATROL.
LOOK AT THE MIRACLE OF GOD'S WORK
REMINDING US, HE'S STILL IN CONTROL.

ca. 2003

THE GENTLE DUKE

MEET CALVIN, THE GENTLE DUKE.
PREPARE FOR THE STARTLING REVELATION,
HIS PERSONA ENIGMA IS EVIDENT.

IT IS OVERWHELMING.
SPEND TIME WITH HIM.
THERE IS A HUNCH,
YOU WILL BE TOUCHED.
TO KNOW HIM IS DELIGHTFUL.
NOTICE THOSE DAZZLING EYES,
HUE OF A DARK DYE.
GAZE INTO THEM;
THEY CAN HYPNOTIZE.

A GENUINE DEVOTIONAL CHRISTIAN,
LEARN OF HIS SALVATION.
HE'S A VOCALIST EXTRAORDINAIRE.
LISTEN TO HIS GOSPEL RENDITIONS,
A MUST IS HIS SOULFUL ARIA.

HE RADIATES BEAUTY AMIDST HIS SURROUNDINGS,
DEPICTING A DEGREE OF GRACIOUSNESS.
HIS CHARM, EXCEPTIONALLY ENCHANTING,
PERSONALITY, EXQUISITELY ELECTRIFYING,
AN OBVIOUS TENDERNESS CERTIFYING.
HIS GRACEFULNESS, ENGULFING,
HIS WARMTH, MAGNIFYING,
RECOGNIZE HIS GENTILITY.

HE EXEMPLIFIES LOVE AND CARING.
AN EXCEPTIONAL FRIEND,
AN INEXHAUSTIBLE STUDENT,
AN IDEAL CITIZEN WITH PASSION,
AN EXTRAORDINARY PERSEVERER,
A LEADER, EXUDING COMPASSION,
AN EXCEEDINGLY ABUNDANCE OF ZEST.

THIS, AND MUCH MORE EPITOMIZES
CALVIN DUPREE, THE GENTLE DUKE.

ca. 2001

THE PAIN KEPT COMING

APPROACHING THE FINAL FLIGHT OF STAIRS,
REALIZED THEY WERE WET FROM THE RAIN
DESCENDING, DISCOVERED THEIR SLIPPERINESS,
GRABBING THE HAND RAILING, CONTINUING DOWNWARD
INSTANTANEOUSLY REPOSITIONING MY GRIP,
NEVERTHELESS, AMAZINGLY, FOUND MYSELF FALLING.

AS I FELL UPON THE CONCRETE LANDING,
HYSTERICALLY AWARE OF THE CRACKLING SOUND,
I KNEW IT WASN'T THE SOUND OF FIRE CRACKERS!
MOMENTARILY, STARS OF NUMEROUS COLORS VISIBLE
THEN, WHEN ATTEMPTING TO RISE
THIS AWESOME, SEVERE PAIN BECAME
EXTREMELY DIFFICULT FOR ME TO ENDURE.
REALIZING I HAD TO GET UP AND CONTINUE,
THOUGH VEHEMENTLY, THE PAIN KEPT COMING.
GRADUALLY, I PULLED MYSELF UPON ONE WOBBLY LEG
UNABLE TO PRESS WEIGHT ON MY LEFT FOOT.
WITH THE AID OF MY UMBRELLA AS A CANE,
I DELICATELY HOBBLED ON MY PAINFUL WAY
AS THE PAIN KEPT COMING.

ARRIVING AT THE EMERGENCY ROOM,
LEARNED I WAS IN FULL SHOCK!
MY BODY TREMBLING FROM THE CHILL,
AS I WAITED FOR ASSISTANCE,
AS I WAITED FOR COMFORT,
AS I WAITED FOR SOME RELIEF,
THE PAIN KEPT COMING.

LATER, RATHER THAN SOONER,
SLOWLY, SERVICES STARTED,
FIRST ONE AND THEN ANOTHER
FINALLY, ONE X-RAY, THEN ANOTHER
THEN, THE DEVASTATING NEWS ARRIVED,
ALL BONES BROKEN IN MY LEFT ANKLE,
WHILE THE PAIN KEPT COMING.

THE LONG, LONG-NEEDED MORPHINE,
SLOWLY COMFORT BEGAN TO BE REALIZED,
BUT THE RELIEF WAS SHORT LIVED.
SADLY, THE GRUESOME PAIN WAS RETURNING,
AND THE PAIN KEPT COMING.

FEBRUARY 2005

THE SAD YOUNG MAN

I MET A YOUNG MAN TODAY.
FROM THE LOOK ON HIS FACE,
I COULD SAY,
TODAY, THIS YOUNG MAN WAS SAD.
DON'T ASK ME WHY,
ALL I CAN SAY,
TODAY, THIS YOUNG MAN WAS SAD.

HE DID NOT SAY MUCH
TO ME WHILE IN THE PAD.
BUT I COULD TELL.
TODAY, THIS YOUNG MAN WAS SAD.
HE WAS NOT A LAD THAT WAS BAD.
YET I WAS AWARE,
TODAY, THIS YOUNG MAN WAS SAD.

HIS EYES GAVE THE SECRET OF THE LAD.
TODAY, THIS YOUNG MAN WAS SAD.
TRUTH BE KNOWN,
THIS YOUNG LAD
REMAINS SAD NOT ONLY TODAY,
BUT, EVERY DAY, HE IS SAD.
PERHAPS . . . THE NEXT TIME,
I WILL FIND OUT WHY HE IS SAD.

ca. 2000

THE SILENCE OF OZZIE

OZZIE IS NOW SILENT, LEAVING US IN SORROW.
IT NEVER OCCURRED THE DAY WOULD ARRIVE
WHEN THE SILENCING OF OZZIE PROCLAIMED,
GONE, THE AMPLIFICATION OF HIS VOICE.
NO LONGER THE AUDIBILITY OF HIS ARTICULATION,
LOST, THE IDENTIFIABLE OF HIS UNIQUE TONE.
NO MORE, THE DETECTING OF HIS DEEP RESONANCE.
EXTINGUISHED THE WARM AND FRIENDLY PERSONA.

THE SILENCE OF OZZIE NOW LEAVES A VOID.
THE ESSENCE OF HIS SUPERBNESS PRESENTED
THE HARSH REALITIES HE OFTEN PASSIONATELY RECITED,
THE FREQUENT SUBTLE REMINDER OF OUR BLACKNESS
ONLY OZZIE COULD DO, MAKING US PROUD.
HE MAGNIFICENTLY ARTICULATED THE ISSUES.
WE COULD ALL STAND TALL WITH DIGNITY AND PRIDE.
OZZIE HAD SPOKEN LOUD AND CLEAR FOR ALL TO HEAR.
NOW OZZIE HAS GONE.
THE SILENCE OF OZZIE IS FOREVER!

FEBRUARY 2005

THESE SENIOR YEARS

SEEMINGLY, IT WAS JUST YESTERYEAR
WE WERE YOUNG, WHIMSICAL, AND CAREFREE.
ASTONISHINGLY, YEARS HAVE SWIFTLY PASSED.
ULTIMATELY, THESE SENIOR YEARS HAVE ARRIVED.

REFLECTING BACK ON SOME HIGHLIGHTS PERSISTING,
THE DECADE OF OUR TWENTIES PRESENTED
CONTINUING OUR MILITARY REQUIREMENTS,
COMPLETING HIGHER EDUCATION FOR SOME,
THERE IS THE ENTRANCE INTO MATRIMONY,
DELIBERATELY SEARCHING FOR A CAPABLE CAREER
AND THE EMERGENCE OF EXPANDING FAMILIES.

THEN THE DECADE OF THE THIRTIES ARRIVED
FOCUSING ON OUR CAREER ADVANCEMENTS,
DEALING WITH VARIOUS FAMILY CRISES,
INVESTMENT IN NEW HOME OWNERSHIPS,
PREPARING CHILDREN FOR CAREER CHOICES.

AMAZINGLY, WE REACHED THE FORTIES DECADE
REALIZING, THEY SAY, "LIFE BEGINS AT FORTY"
CHILDREN LEAVING THEIR NEST FOR COLLEGES,
SOME FINDING MARRIAGE OVER. SINGLE AGAIN.
SOME ENTERING ANOTHER MARRIAGE ONCE MORE.

THE FIFTIES DECADE ARRIVED WITH GREAT CONCERNS.
THERE WERE DISSOLUTIONS OF MANY CAREERS,
PROVIDING ASSISTANCE WITH GRANDCHILDREN,
RECOGNIZING THE BEGINNING OF ACHES AND PAINS,
INVESTIGATING OUR RETIREMENT OPPORTUNITIES.

UNBELIEVABLY, WE REACHED THE SIXTIES DECADE.
REALIZATION OF FIFTY YEARS OUT OF HIGH SCHOOL,
SOME ACCEPTING THEIR SENIOR CITIZEN STATUS,
OUR RETIREMENT BECOMES A PARAMOUNT ISSUE,
THE ACHES AND PAINS CONTINUE TO BUILD.

AH, THE SEVENTIES DECADE IS UPON US!
DEEP INTO THESE SENIOR YEARS OF OURS,
ONE DOCTOR APPOINTMENT AFTER ANOTHER,
SOME BEST FRIENDS HAVE MADE THEIR TRANSITION,
SOME TRAVELING TO PLACES UNKNOWN OR UNVISITED.

NOW, WE FIND OURSELVES HERE CELEBRATING
THE FIFTY-FIVE YEARS SINCE CARDOZO HIGH SCHOOL.
RECOGNIZING ALL THE NUMEROUS ACCOLADES,
ACCOMPLISHMENTS, AND AWARDS ACHIEVED BY US.
YET WE MAY ASK, COULD WE HAVE DONE IT ANY DIFFERENTLY.
PLEASED, WE ARE STILL HERE ENJOYING THE FELLOWSHIP
AND EXCITEMENT OF THE YEARS WE ALL STILL HAVE LEFT!

ca. 2009

THIS NIGHT

THIS NIGHT, I LIE AWAKE
AWARE OF MY AWKWARD DILEMMA.
THIS NIGHT, IT IS ALL ABOUT WONDERING
THIS NIGHT, AWARE OF THE STORMINESS
SHALL THIS BE CAUSE FOR ALARM?

LYING HERE, CAUSING IRRATIONAL CONFUSION.
ONE THING, THERE IS NO ACT OF COERCION
THOUGH THERE IS AN ATTEMPT IN GRASPING,
WHILE THERE ARE EFFORTS OF EXTENDED JOKING.

LYING HERE, BEING UNEQUIVOCALLY DEFIANT;
IT IS TRUE, THERE IS NO SIGN OF CARING.
THERE IS NO INDICATION OF FEELINGS.
THIS NIGHT, LYING HERE, HIGHLY STRESSED,
COGNIZANT OF MY ILLOGICAL INEPTNESS,
THIS NIGHT, I CONTINUE MY PONDERING.

ca. 2008

THIS TROUBLED WORLD

THIS TROUBLED WORLD
SHOULD CAUSE ONE TO PAUSE.
TAKE TIME TO NOTICE GLOBAL ISSUES
CONSTANTLY ARE BOMBARDED WITH DANGER.
THERE IS ONE CRISIS AFTER ANOTHER
AWARENESS OF THE CALAMITIES OF EVENTS
CRISIS MADE BY MAN OR BY NATURE,
THESE DISASTERS THAT ARE AFFECTING US
IN THIS TROUBLED WORLD.

EVENTS THAT BRING ABOUT CAUSE AND EFFECTS.
THERE ARE AIR—AND WATER-POLLUTION PROBLEMS.
NO LONGER CAN THESE PROBLEMS BE IGNORED,
WHETHER IT IS GLOBAL WARMING,
POSSIBLY A TSUNAMI, CAUSING FLOODING
THAT CAN LEAD TO POTENTIAL MUD SLIDINGS,
OR WHETHER IT IS AN INJURIOUS DROUGHT
IN THIS TROUBLED WORLD.

NATURE PRESENTING DEVASTATING HURRICANES,
YET IT COULD BE A DESTRUCTIVE TORNADO,
ARSONIST, OR LIGHTNING, CAUSING HAZARDOUS FIRES,
CONSTANTLY PREDICTIONS OF A SEVERE EARTHQUAKE,
ACTIVATION OF A DEVASTATING EXPELLING VOLCANO.
THERE ARE CONSTANTLY CATASTROPHIC SNOWSTORMS
IN THIS TROUBLED WORLD.

MAN CREATES CRISES OF WARS,
CONDITIONS CREATE EXTREME FAMINE,
PROBLEMS DEALING WITH MAN'S GENOCIDE,
LEADERS IGNORING THE PROBLEM OF HIV/AIDS,
COUNTRIES DISREGARD BORDER BOUNDARIES,
INTOLERANCE IGNORED BETWEEN RELIGIOUS SECTS,
IN THIS TROUBLED WORLD.

TIME IS OF ESSENCE IN THIS TROUBLED WORLD.
WE NEED TO TAKE CAUSE TO PAUSE;
MANKIND OF THE WORLD MUST ALL TAKE NOTICE;
THIS TROUBLED WORLD REQUIRES PRAYER FROM ALL.
THIS TROUBLED WORLD NEEDS CHANGES
BEFORE IT BECOMES TOO LATE FOR
THIS TROUBLED WORLD.

ca. 2006

TIME

WHERE HAS MY TIME GONE?
YESTERDAY, I REMEMBER
THE DREAMS I HELD DEARLY,
TIME WAS PLENTIFUL,
DREAMS FULFILLED CLEARLY,
ON *TIME*.

IDEAS CREATED,
ACCOMPLISHED ON *TIME*.
THOUGHTS DEVELOPED,
COMPLETED NEARLY ON *TIME*.
PLANS ESTABLISHED,
FOR A DUE *TIME*.
DEEDS UNDERTAKEN,
FOR A CERTAIN *TIME*.

MY, MY, *TIME* IS FLEETING!
TODAY, GOALS ARE NEEDED:
SHORT ONES,
I HAVE *TIME*;
INTERMEDIATE ONES,
I WILL FIND *TIME*;
LONG-RANGE ONES,
HOPEFULLY, I WILL HAVE *TIME*.

WHERE HAS MY *TIME* GONE?
JUST YESTERDAY,
I DREAMED OF MY FUTURE.
NOW, MY FUTURE IS HERE!
WHERE DID MY *TIME* GO?

PLEASE TELL ME, HOW MUCH *TIME*
I HAVE BEFORE TOMORROW,
WHEN IT'S MY *TIME* TO GO.

ca. 1999

TO KNOW ME

YOU KNOW I'M SMART, I'M YOUNG, I'M DUMB.
    TIME WITH ME IS DUBIOUS
        ALLOWS YOU ASK PERTINENT QUESTIONS.
           IF I RESPOND TRUTHFULLY,
               YOU WILL WANT TO KNOW ME.

YOU KNOW I'M SMART, I'M YOUNG, I'M DUMB.
    MANIPULATION WORKS FOR WHAT I WANT.
        ALLOWS YOU TO CHARM ME
           I NEED NOT BE RESPONSIVE,
               SINCE YOU WANT TO KNOW ME.

YOU KNOW I'M SMART, I'M YOUNG, I'M DUMB.
    USE ABILITIES ONLY WHEN NECESSARY.
        SAVE MYSELF FOR OTHER MATTERS,
           LEARNED YOU'LL RESCUE ME.
               IT WILL ALLOW YOU TO KNOW ME.

YOU KNOW I'M SMART, I'M YOUNG, I'M DUMB.
    SPEND QUALITY TIME WITH ME,
        LISTEN TO ME OBJECTIVELY,
           OFFER INTELLIGENT ADVICE,
               WILL ENABLE YOU TO KNOW ME.

YOU KNOW I'M SMART, I'M YOUNG, I'M DUMB.
    WHY USE MY INTELLECTUAL BRAIN?
        WHY USE MY PRECIOUS PHYSICAL ENERGY?
           LESS PROVIDED, THE MORE YOU'LL OFFER,
               AFTER ALL, YOU WANT TO KNOW ME.

YOU KNOW I'M SMART, I'M YOUNG, I'M DUMB.
    ENJOY WATCHING YOU DOING FOR ME.
        INDICATIONS ARE, YOU ARE WILLING,
           THEN, WHY NOT LET YOU,
               REALIZING YOU WANT TO KNOW ME.

YOU KNOW I'M SMART, I'M YOUNG, I'M DUMB.
THOSE THAT DON'T PROVIDE FOR ME,
I HAVE NO USE FOR THEM.
LET THEM GO THEIR WAY
WHILE I'LL CONTINUE ON MINE.
COME ALONG, YOU WANT TO
KNOW ME.

YOU KNOW I'M SMART, I'M YOUNG, I'M DUMB.
USE MY TIME FOR CHILLING.
MY TIME SPENT WITH FRIENDS.
MY TIME DOING NOTHING RELEVANT.
STILL, YOU WANT TO KNOW ME.

YOU KNOW I'M SMART, I'M YOUNG, I'M DUMB.
DON'T NEED TO ANSWER YOUR INTERROGATIONS.
DON'T NEED TO LISTEN TO YOU.
DON'T NEED YOUR HASSELS.
DON'T NEED YOUR INTERRUPTIONS.
NEVERTHELESS, YOU WANT TO
KNOW ME.

YOU KNOW I'M SMART, I'M YOUNG, I'M DUMB.
DON'T NEED TO DO ANYTHING I DON'T WANT,
WON'T OFFER MY WILLINGNESS.
WON'T AGREE WITH YOUR REQUESTS.
AFTER ALL, I CAN ALWAYS GO HOME!
THEN, YOU WON'T GET TO
KNOW ME.

ca. 2002

WAKE UP, BROTHERS AND SISTERS

WAKE UP, BROTHERS AND SISTERS,
YOU'VE SLEPT LONG ENOUGH.
THIS IS NO TIME FOR SLEEPING.
YOU'VE LOST SIGNIFICANT RIGHTS,
INJUSTICES ARE HEAPING UPON YOU.
I SAY, WAKE UP! WAKE UP!
THERE IS MUCH TO BE DONE.
IF YOU WANT TO PREVENT FURTHER EROSION,
HURRY, GET UP BEFORE IT'S TOO LATE.

WAKE UP, BROTHERS AND SISTERS,
WHILE YOU WERE SLEEPING,
YOU'VE BEEN SORROWFULLY UNAWARE
THE HORRENDOUS CALAMITY THAT EXISTS.
I SAY, WAKE UP! WAKE UP!
NO MORE HIGHER EDUCATION.
THERE'S ERODING OF YOUR OPPORTUNITIES:
THERE'S ELIMINATING OF QUALITY POSITIONS.
YOU'RE NOT CONSIDERED FOR PROMOTIONS.

WAKE UP, BROTHERS AND SISTERS,
YOU'VE SLEPT LONG ENOUGH.
YOU ARE ABOUT TO LOSE YOUR JOB.
YOU ARE ABOUT TO DISCOVER HOMELESSNESS.
YOU'LL DISCOVER YOUR NEST EGG'S GONE.
YOUR FAMILIES ARE BEING INCARCERATED.
YOUR KINFOLK ARE SENSELESSLY MURDERED.
I SAY, WAKE UP! WAKE UP!
SOME ACCUSED OF HIGH CRIMES AND TREASON.
WAKE UP, BROTHERS AND SISTERS,
HURRY, GET UP BEFORE IT'S TOO LATE.

ca. 2003

WHERE ARE WE GOING?

WHERE ARE WE GOING?
TO WHAT ARE WE COMING?
CORPORATIONS CONCERNED WITH GREED,
INDEPENDENT COMPANIES DEVOURED BY CONGLOMERATES,
MOM AND POP ESTABLISHMENTS LITERALLY ELIMINATED,
RICH INDIVIDUALS STEALING IN ABUNDANCE,
THE MIDDLE CLASS DEMANDING MORE,
WHILE POOR PEOPLE RECEIVING LESS.

WHERE ARE WE GOING?
TO WHAT ARE WE COMING?
RACE RELATIONS CONTINUE DETERIORATING,
GENDER AGAINST GENDER MUSTER CHALLENGES,
OLD FOLK DESPISED BY YOUTHS,
YOUTHS MISUNDERSTOOD BY THEIR ELDERS,
FIRE PROTECTORS IDENTIFIED AS ARSONISTS,
POLICE PERSONS FOUND GUILTY OF CRIMES.

WHERE ARE WE GOING?
TO WHAT ARE WE COMING?
MANY COMMUNITIES DISENCHANTED,
WILLINGNESS TO SUCCEED FROM CITIES,
CITIES DISENFRANCHISED WITH THEIR STATE,
STATES DEMANDING MORE FEDERAL ASSISTANCE,
NATIONS FIGHTING NATIONS FOR LAND AND POWER,
COUNTRIES STRUGGLING OVER BORDERS.

WHERE ARE WE GOING?
TO WHAT ARE WE COMING?
OUR ADMINISTRATION CONTROLLED
BY THE RELIGIOUS RIGHT EXTREMISTS.
POLITICIANS ONLY INTERESTED IN OUR VOTE.
COURT SYSTEMS TAINTED BY SPECIAL INTERESTS.
SEGMENTS OF OUR POPULATION BECOME HOMELESS.
WE BUILD MORE JAILS FOR THE INCARCERATED.

WHERE ARE WE GOING?
TO WHAT ARE WE COMING?
AVERAGE FAMILIES LEFT BEHIND.
MANY REQUIRED TO WORK TWO JOBS,
LEAVING LESS TIME WITH FAMILIES.
HOUSING TOTALLY OUT OF THEIR RANGE.
COST OF LIVING NOT KIND TO OUR POOR PEOPLE.
HEALTH CARE VIRTUALLY NON-EXISTENT FOR MANY.

WHERE ARE WE GOING?
TO WHAT ARE WE COMING?
VICTIMS CONSTANTLY BEING BRUTALIZED.
SOME PARENTS IGNORING THEIR RESPONSIBILITIES.
ADULTS MOLESTING CHILDREN FOR PLEASURE,
SOME BURGLARIZING, OTHERS INFLICTING PAIN.
SOME COMMIT HOMICIDES WITHOUT CONSCIOUSNESS.
SUBSTANCE ABUSE RUNNING RAMPANT IN NEIGHBORHOODS.

WHERE ARE WE GOING?
TO WHAT ARE WE COMING?
CITIES DETERIORATING RIGHT BEFORE US.
INNER CITY INFRASTRUCTURE NOT AT PACE,
WITH OUR CITIES' POPULATION.
OUR BEACHES CONSTANTLY POLLUTED.
THE ATMOSPHERE RAPIDLY DETERIORATING.
NEIGHBORHOODS IN DIRE NEED OF REVITALIZATION.

WHERE ARE WE GOING?
TO WHAT ARE WE COMING?
OUR COUNTRY FOUNDED ON BRUTALITY.
YET WE HAVE SAID, "IN GOD WE TRUST"
SOME FIGHT AGAINST ACKNOWLEDGMENT
ANY SIGNS OF RELIGIOUS BELIEFS AND SYMBOLS
CHARGING SEPARATION RELIGION AND GOVERNMENT.

WHERE ARE WE GOING?
TO WHAT ARE WE COMING?
ESTABLISHMENTS ALLOWING EDUCATION UTILIZED
BY THE UNDOCUMENTED, AT EXPENSE OF CITIZENS,
EDUCATION OUT OF THE REACH OF MANY,
COLLEGE COSTS EXCESSIVELY FOR AVERAGE STUDENTS,
WITHOUT AN EDUCATION, NO JOBS AVAILABLE,
AS JOBS ARE SENT TO OTHER COUNTRIES.

WHERE ARE WE GOING?
TO WHAT ARE WE COMING?
DISEASES ELIMINATING MANY PEOPLE,
AIDS COSTING MANY LIVES,
OBESITY ON THE RISE AMONG YOUNG,
DIABETES INCREASING AT AN ALARMING RATE,
CANCERS PARTICULARLY TAKING THEIR TOLL,
ALZHEIMER'S TRAGEDY DESTROYING SENIORS.

NO WONDER WE ARE ASKING,
WHERE ARE WE GOING?
TO WHAT ARE WE COMING?

ca. 2004

YOU DON'T REALLY KNOW ME

THERE IS CONSTANT CONDEMNATION OF ME.
BUT, HAVE YOU EVER WALKED IN MY SHOES?
HAVE YOU EVER LAIN IN MY BED?
HAVE YOU EVER TALKED WITH ME,
NOT TALKED AT ME?
THEN, YOU DON'T REALLY KNOW ME.

HAVE YOU EVER BEEN BLATANTLY REFUSED?
HAVE YOU EXPERIENCED MY SORDID REJECTIONS
BECAUSE OF WHOM I AM?
HAVE YOU EVER SHARED MY NUMEROUS ANXIETIES?
HAVE YOU EXPERIENCED MY LIMITLESS DISAPPOINTMENTS
DUE TO YOUR COLOR?
THEN, YOU DON'T REALLY KNOW ME.

HAVE YOU EVER BEEN RELEGATED TO THE BACK?
HAVE YOU EVER BEEN FORCIBLY BRUTALIZED?
HAVE YOU EVER BEEN DECLARED UNQUALIFIED
BY ONE FAR LESS COMPETENT THAN YOU?
IF YOU HAVE NOT HAD THESE EXPERIENCES,
THEN, YOU DON'T REALLY KNOW ME.

HISTORICALLY, PSYCHOLOGICALLY, SOCIOLOGICALLY,
WE CAN DEDUCE YOU DON'T REALLY KNOW ME.
THEN, YOU NEED TO REFRAIN
FROM YOUR CONDEMNATION OF ME.

ca. 2004

YOUR NAME

FROM THE DAY WE WERE JOINED
I WAS GIVEN YOUR NAME.
EVER SINCE THAT DAY
I HAVE GIVEN UP MY INDEPENDENCE.
AS A RESULT OF REGAINING MY SELF-RELIANCE
NOW, I DON'T WANT YOUR NAME.

SINCE I RECEIVED YOUR NAME
I HAVE HAD TO LIVE YOUR LIFE.
I INDULGED IN YOUR ASPIRATIONS.
I HAVE HAD TO LIVE YOUR DREAMS.
I HAVE HAD TO FULFILL YOUR HOPES.
I HAVE HAD TO STRIDE IN YOUR PRIDE.
NOW, I DON'T WANT YOUR NAME.

SINCE LIVING IN YOUR LIFE
I NEVER OBTAINED MY GOALS.
I NEVER REALIZED MY DREAMS.
I NEVER ACQUIRED MY ASPIRATIONS.
NOW YOU WANT ME TO DUTIFULLY
CONTINUE TO CARRY YOUR NAME.
NO, I DON'T WANT YOUR NAME.

YOU DON'T WANT ME TO EVER
OBTAIN MY DESIRED GOALS.
NOR REALIZE MY ASPIRATIONS
OR FULFILL MY DREAMS AND HOPES.
ALL BECAUSE OF YOUR NAME.
NO LONGER WILL I USE YOUR NAME.
I WILL TAKE BACK MY NAME.
I DON'T WANT YOUR NAME!

ca. 2004

DEATH

DEATH IS TRULY SWIRLING
ALL AROUND ME.

FIRST, IT'S WHIRLING ON MY
IMMEDIATE RIGHT.

THERE IT GOES,
TWIRLING ON MY EXTREME LEFT.

NOW, HERE IT IS, BRINGING DELIBERATE
HAVOC RIGHT BEFORE ME.

WATCH OUT, FOR I FEEL,
DEATH IS SLOWLY CREEPING UP BEHIND ME.

DEATH HAS QUIETLY CREPT UPON MANY A FRIEND.

DEATH HAS RAPIDLY SEIZED MANY LOVED ONES.

DEATH HAS COME TO SOME WITH A SUDDEN BANG.

DEATH HAS ALSO COME SOFTLY AND GENTLY.

BUT, DEATH HAS EVEN GIVEN WARNINGS.

OH DEATH, OH DARKNESS OF DEATH,

OH CRUEL DEATH, OH QUIET AND GENTLE DEATH,

I WONDER HOW DEATH WILL SNATCH THE NEXT.

ca. 2004

INDEX OF FIRST LINES

A

B

C

D

E

EMPEROR KING NOBLY STANDS BEFORE ME, 31

F

FOR ALL THE CONTINUOUS HOURS, 52
FROM THE DAY WE WERE JOINED, 115

G

"GOOD-BYE", 35

H

HE QUIETLY ARRIVED AT THE ENTRANCE, 76
HERE, AMIDST MY REFLECTIONS, 57
HERE IN THE MIDST OF THE WWII MEMORIAL, 23
HE STOOD, HE LISTENED, 36

I

IF THIS EMOTIONAL DESIRE PERSISTS, 79
I MET A YOUNG MAN TODAY, 100
IN MOMENTS OF PAIN, YOU'RE HERE, 37
IN OUR WORLD OF TODAY, 73
IN THE CHARM OF SPRINGTIME, 45
IN THE DEEP, DEEP, DEEP, 81
IN THE QUIET OF THE MORNING, 46
IN THESE HOURS OF REMINISCING, 59
IN THE SUPREME PRESENCE OF SIR FRANK, 92
IN TIMES OF DESPAIR, 66
I RAISE MY VOICE IN FEAR, 58
IT IS INEVITABLE, THERE IS NO ESCAPING, 27
I TRUST THE GENTLE FRAGRANCE THAT FILLS THE AIR, 30
I WONDER, 42
I WONDER WHY, 43

J

JOHN JOHN, A CHARISMATIC, DEBONAIR YOUNG MAN, 48

L

LADIES AND GENTLEMEN, FRIEND OR FOE, 72
LIFE, I BREATHE INTO IT, 13
LISTENING TO SONGS GIVES GREAT JOY, 93

M

MANY START PURSUING THEIR LIFE'S JOURNEY, 21
MEET CALVIN, THE GENTLE DUKE, 97
MERCY, MERCY ME, 55
MOTHER, NOW AS YOU LIE IN PEACE, 70
MY CELLOPHANE PRINCE, 56
MY SISTER, MY SISTER, 67

O

OCCASIONALLY, 17
OH, HUMAN BEINGS OF THE WORLD, PRAY, 75
OZZIE IS NOW SILENT, LEAVING US IN SORROW, 101

P

PEERING OUT AT THE SHADES OF CLOUDS, 89
PRINCE DANIEL, KNOWN AS THE NUMBER ONE, 77

R

REMINISCING WHILE GAZING AT THE SEA, 18
RICH WHITE WOMEN'S AUDACITY IS AMAZING, 85

S

SEEMINGLY, IT WAS JUST YESTERYEAR, 102
SINCE LADY ANNIE'S TRANSITION, 49
SITTING BY THE WINDOW, 96
SOCIETY IS MAD WITH SELFISHNESS, 88

T

TAKE NOTE, SOCIETY IS FULL OF PRANCERS, 74
THERE IS A TIME FOR EVERYTHING, 41

CPSIA information can be obtained at www.ICGtesting.com
Printed in the USA
BVOW05s1302080614

355650BV00001B/74/P

9 781456 853358